THE UPSIDE OF DOWNSIZING

USING LIBRARY INSTRUCTION TO COPE

Edited by
Cheryl LaGuardia, Stella Bentley, and Janet Martorana

Neal-Schuman Publishers, Inc.

New York   London

Published by Neal-Schuman Publishers, Inc.
100 Varick Street
New York, NY 10013

Library of Congress Cataloging-in-Publication Data

The upside of downsizing : using library instruction to cope /
edited
  by Cheryl LaGuardia, Stella Bentley and Janet Martorana
      p.   cm.
  Papers presented at a conference held at the University of
California at Santa Barbara.
  Includes bibliographical references (p.   ) and index.
  ISBN 1-55570-217-1
  1. Academic libraries—Reference services—United States—
Congresses. 2. Library orientation—United States—Congresses.
I. LaGuardia, Cheryl.
Z675.U5U67   1995
025.5'677'0973—dc20   95-13157
                                                        CIP

Table of Contents

Acknowledgments

As anyone who's ever held a conference knows, the success of the enterprise is dependent on the hard work of many people. We were fortunate to have many exceptional contributions to our conference and we'd like to acknowledge these here.

To conference presenters and attendees, we send our warmest thanks for making the results of a year's labor so stimulating and rewarding. Thank you, Carla Stoffle, for your gracious early acceptance of our invitation to keynote the conference. Thanks also to Barbara Quint and Janice Simmons-Welburn for your early sign-ons to participate (which caught the attention of many who were hearing about the conference by word of mouth).

Martin Raish (BI-L list moderator): thank you for making available and maintaining such a vital library instruction resource—the response to our call for papers on BI-L was tremendous.

We wish also to thank Joseph Boisse, Joanne Euster, and Gloria Werner for serving as a spontaneous expert reactor panel for the keynote speech. The discussion was a lively one: unfortunately, its very interactive, dynamic nature precluded its appearance in the printed proceedings. Although their format also precludes our including them in the proceedings, the conference poster sessions were very well-received and we'd like to thank those presenters for their participation in the conference: Sharon O. Geltner, Philip C. Howze, Chuck Huber, Kelly Janousek, Janet Martorana, Lucia Snowhill, Eileen Wakiji, and Linda Weber.

Many thanks to the UCSB Conference Planning and Implementation Committee for the work they put into making the conference such a success: Christine Oka (Associate Conference Chair), Rosemary Meszaros (Registration), Patrick Dawson (Local Arrangements), Andrea Duda (Publicity), John Vasi (Finance), Carolbeth Gibbens (Moderators), Chuck Huber (Poster Sessions), Adan Griego (Speaker Liaison), and Joe Boisse (Friends Liaison). Special thanks from the Conference Committee to the Friends of the UCSB Library for cosponsoring the conference.

Thanks also to the UCSB librarian volunteers who moderated sessions and made the process run so smoothly: Detrice Bankhead, Yolanda Blue, Barbara Ceizler Silver, Weiling Dai, Sherry DeDecker, Carol Doyle, Sylvelin Edgerton, Cecily Johns, Lisa Melendez (formerly at UCSB), Lucia Snowhill, and Sally Weimer.

My personal thanks to Esther Grassian and Ilene Rockman for kindly stepping in at the last minute and moderating conference sessions. I am deeply indebted to you both.

Cheryl LaGuardia

One Little Conference and How It Grew: An Introduction

Cheryl LaGuardia
Conference Co-Chair
Coordinator of the Electronic Teaching Center,
Harvard University
(formerly at the University of California at Santa Barbara)

It's a very pleasant surprise to be writing this introduction to the proceedings of our conference on library instruction—a surprise because, frankly, the conference was originally planned as a small, regional seminar only, for academic librarians in the Southwest (California, Nevada, Arizona). Like Topsy, however, it just grew and grew.

We undertook the conference because of the considerable downsizing we experienced at UCSB over a period of several years. The number of librarians was reduced practically by half, yet we continued for several years to try to offer the same services, as well as the same level of services, as when we were fully staffed.

Couldn't be done! as anyone reading this knows full well. Yet, we were convinced that effective strategies for coping within the new downsized environment did exist. We came up with a few on our own, including the revitalization of our library instruction program and consolidation of service points—but we were confident there were many more tactics out there to be made use of. What better way to learn about these than to have people come to Santa Barbara and, in effect, deliver them to us personally? Planning for the conference began immediately thereafter. . . .

We put out a call for papers on BI-L, and almost at once discovered we needed to reassess our plans for scope: we were getting responses from as far away as the Bodleian Library in Oxford, England! Admittedly, some of these were only notes of interest in the conference topic, but enough replies came in from around the country and Canada to convince us that we'd be wrong to limit participation to only a couple of western states. Suddenly we had a national (actually, international with the Canadian participation) event on our hands. We eventually received proposals from 45 states and Canada.

As we were expanding the scope of the conference, we took another look at its length. Originally a one-day meeting was planned, but if we were going to bring in people from the East Coast we concluded a day-and-a-half-long conference would be more reasonable. (We had to draw the line somewhere in terms of local arrangements: so many excellent presentation proposals came in from BI-L that we could easily have had a three- or four-day meeting.)

A Deep, Abiding, and *Growing* Interest

Anyone involved in library instruction knows that there is enormous interest in sharing the tricks of the trade: this is standard operating procedure for instruction librarians, as the dynamic existence of such instructional groups as LOEX and CCLI (the California Clearinghouse for Library Instruction) attests. It was clear to us that by considering instruction within the context of downsizing we'd tapped into TWO areas of major interest for librarians nationwide. After all, who's *expanding* staff these days? Who wasn't going to want to hear what was said at this conference?

Witness the high attendance (we reached full capacity for the local facility) and attendees' enthusiastic response to the conference. We were fortunate to have with us an extraordinary group of individuals, both as presenters and attendee participants, and the level of excitement and sense of shared purpose at the conference was communicated even to those of us on the Planning and Implementation Committee who were slightly numb from putting the whole thing together.

What follows is the substance of the all-conference and breakout session papers delivered at the "Upside of Downsizing" conference. Papers have been edited to remove obvious "speech-ese," but otherwise are presented pretty much as we heard them. I hope you enjoy and learn as much from these proceedings as we did in putting on the conference.

1

The Upside of Downsizing: Using the Economic Crisis to Restructure and Revitalize Academic Libraries

Carla Stoffle
University of Arizona

Before we can talk about the upside of downsizing (a euphemism for making budget reductions as positive as possible), understand the context for the downsizing. To do that we must understand what is happening in higher education in general and to our libraries in particular. What we are about is not a temporary reduction in funding or a temporary shift in the way we do business. We are about a fundamental restructuring of the library's budget that will force a restructuring of what we do, how we do it, and how we are organized to do it. The key work of the library, and the focus of library activity, will have to change if libraries are to be an essential part of higher education in the future. We must accept, and embrace, this challenge. To set the stage for the rest of the instructional program, I will review the budget climate that drives the need for fundamental change; what kind of changes are necessary; why the educational role of the academic library will emerge as fundamental to accomplishing our mission; and why instruction librarians are likely to lead the way in making necessary changes.

THE STATUS OF HIGHER EDUCATION

Public support for higher education has been at an unprecedented high for nearly 50 years. For the most part there were huge influxes of funds—tax dollars, federal research grants, private giving, and/or tuition—to support expansion of programs, staff, and buildings. The few down periods over this time usually lasted for two or three years at the outside. For the most part, the down periods were marked with flat budgets rather than reductions in already allocated funds. Where reductions occurred, they were usually tied to decreased student enrollments, and even these tended to be cyclical rather than permanent. Universal access to higher education was the public policy goal, and funding generally followed that policy.

For most of us who came into higher education during this period, it would be easy to assume that this pattern of funding was the norm, and thus the economic downturn in funding of the 1990s is an anomaly that will soon pass. All we have to do is to hold on long enough, and good times—or at least better times—will return. We need only do what we have done in the past—hunker down, trim around the edges, freeze positions, reduce maintenance and operations budgets, eliminate equipment purchases, etc. Then things will return to normal and we can return funding to those areas.

The Downturn

However, the current decrease in funding and the general economic climate facing higher education is not like the past. The economy is not expanding and will not expand like it did in the 1960s and 1970s or even the 1980s. Many high-paying jobs have been eliminated and are being replaced by new jobs with lower wages in service industries. Tax revenues, if not down, are not expanding quickly enough to meet the needs for funding. State budgets have had to absorb huge increases in welfare, health, and public safety (prisons) spending. There are simply fewer dollars available to fund higher education.

At the same time, the public has adopted different attitudes about higher education's role and the public good. For the most part, the public is less willing to blindly fund increases even for legislatively mandated new activities, let alone the inflation that is driving higher education cost increases at a greater pace than any other area of the economy except health. The public is questioning how well higher education is meeting its responsibilities. There is a sense that the professorate is out of control and unaccountable—teaching little, producing less in public service, concentrating on personal research, and/or spending time in outside personal consulting to the detriment of the public. There is a growing public perception that there is great waste and fat in our institutions. In addition, higher education is seen as primarily an individual good, increasingly inaccessible to larger segments of the population. Therefore, individuals—students who have access to and will economically benefit from a degree—should assume a larger portion of the cost via tuition and fee increases. Some large increases in tuition and the creation of new fees (e.g., computing) have occurred, but these have not been sufficient to meet institutional needs and have been used in state institutions to replace state funding rather than increase the total dollars available. (In private institutions increased tuition has not kept up with needs either, and its justification is being questioned.)

For institutions relying on the federal research funding that grew exponentially since World War II, federal dollars in the 1990s have become increasingly difficult to obtain. For those getting grants, the most recent scandals about overhead or indirect costs have greatly restricted the amount of money available to support infrastructure—utilities, libraries, staffing to support the grant process, etc.—further increasing pressure on institutions that must now find other sources of funding for these costs. It is likely that research overhead recovery will continue to be restricted rather than return to the former situation, wherein institutional infrastructure costs were covered to a large extent.

Private giving is the one bright spot for many universities and colleges. Giving is up, but it is not generally available for operations and certainly not sufficient to replace other sources of revenue. Also, the competition between public and private institutions for personal and corporate donations is increasing.

While not an inclusive description of the budget situation, the foregoing is intended to illustrate a basic point: The economics of higher education—where money comes from, how much is available, and how it will be spent—is undergoing a paradigm shift. The sharp cuts and flat budgets experienced over the last three or four years will not be undone as we could have expected in the past; in fact, further cuts are likely. Flat budgets will be the norm, with perhaps only small salary increases resulting. Minimal increases for operations and increased staff will be seen as a return to good times. To meet their missions, colleges and universities will have to change the way they do business; reducing or eliminating redundancies within and between institutions along the way. More attention will have to be paid to instruction, especially undergraduate education. The way institutions are managed and how they allocate and spend the budget will have to change. The institutional distortions created by trying to wait out the current recession will have to be undone; infrastructure issues will have to be attended to. Buildings and equipment must be refurbished and replaced, and operations budgets for travel, small equipment, paper, copying, etc., will have to be restored. More dollars will have to be invested in capital-intensive ways—especially the computing and networking infrastructure—and this investment will require constant upgrading, not just one-time funds.

All of the above will mean fewer dollars spent on people. Institutions of higher education will significantly reduce their workforce, including faculty, over the next decade.

The Effect on Academic Libraries

Academic library funding and budget management has often mirrored the institutional situation. When times were good, there were large increases to materials budget—not only to keep up with inflation but also to attempt to capture a larger portion of the world's publishing output. Investment in new buildings to house the collections also meant increased staff to process the materials purchased. In the 1980s, there were even some increases to preservation budgets. Unfortunately, when times got bad, libraries did as their institutions did: cut across the board with the understanding that good times would soon return and the reductions would be restored.

With this philosophy and management style, libraries struggled through the early 1990s, and librarians have come to realize that, as higher education changes, libraries must change. However, factors creating the need for a budget paradigm shift for libraries predate the general economic crisis of the 1990s and make the library situation even more critical. For academic libraries, the budget crisis began in the 1980s, driven by the price increases in scientific/technical journals and the dramatic changes in information technologies requiring more capital investment and increased operational expenditures.

Escalating journal prices were first met by a combination of budget increases from institutional funds and shifts from other parts of the collection budget. Naturally, the collection budget increases came at the expense of other areas. Then it became necessary to cut journals and fund alternative forms of access (the staff, equipment, and operational dollars needed to support interlibrary loan and commercial document delivery). These funds often come from reallocating a number of library sources, including the acquisitions budget.

During this same period, investments in information technologies were often made with one-time funds from institutional sources without the ongoing budget allocation to maintain and replace the equipment. The new technologies open up exciting new possibilities for library service delivery but require a reallocation and reshaping of the library's budget.

The Results of Downsizing

Academic libraries are now at a critical juncture. To cover the combination of new costs and budget decreases, we freeze or eliminate positions and cut at the edges—travel, supplies, equipment, etc. We reduce services—less reference, less instruction, fewer guides and handouts, increased turnaround time for reshelving and technical processing, etc. The library is increasingly organized for the convenience of staff, to make them more effective in serving user needs quickly—but also, ironically, forcing users to become more staff-dependent.

We tinker with the organization, even eliminating a unit here or there. We struggle to maintain the old and to provide the new, doing neither very well. Many of us are on the road of slow decline rather than the road to improvement. Staff are stressed, feeling out of control, overwhelmed, and overworked.

Solving the Problem

Radical, fundamental change is necessary to turn this situation around. We must rethink and rebuild our libraries from the ground up. The radical restructuring of our libraries must focus on adopting a user (customer) focus, committing to quality service—with quality defined by the user—accepting the need for continual change, creating teams rather than departments or individual-based work units, and empowering front-line staff to make the decisions necessary to meet the missions and goals of the library on a daily basis.

As we focus on the needs of our customers, rather than the ownership of collections or the needs of staff, our key work activities, our organizational structure, our services, and even our physical environment will change for the better. Eliminate ''sacred cows'' (those programs and activities that we never questioned) and redundancies born of double-checking work or creating special files just in case a problem occurs. (For example, how many libraries are still maintaining paper files in addition to online systems?) Unleash the creative potential of all staff by stressing teamwork and empowering them to make decisions that get the highest-priority work accomplished. At the same time, reduce the need for hierarchy, allowing us to focus more resources on the front line rather than on management. Open up your organizations to the idea of using fiscal and human resources in the most effective way rather than the "this is how we have always done it" way or the most politically acceptable way.

Increase your organizational flexibility and ability to change as new opportunities and challenges arise. Move more staff into public contact activities and out of the back room increasing our ability to make hard choices because the entire organization will understand the needs (having identified the problems and solutions) and thus will be committed to the results.

At the heart of a user-focused library is the goal of making users self-sufficient in their information seeking and use of libraries. To achieve the goal, there must be a commitment to empower patrons to do as much as they can for themselves without having to go to staff for help. We must be willing to continually review and evaluate services, the physical organization, and the physical environment with the eyes of the users and to make the commitment to removing barriers identified— even if the barrier is us! We must also be committed to conscious design of libraries and information systems for our customers, rather than for librarians.

Before I go further and define user self-sufficiency, be assured that what I am talking about is a goal of user self-sufficiency as a philosophy to guide our efforts. I am not talking about an unwillingness to help users, or removing public staffing, or forcing users to be staff independent.

Conversely, we will never achieve the full goals of self-sufficiency. The information environment is changing too dramatically and will continue to change if society and the economy of the twenty-first century are really going to be information-based. Librarians today cannot even keep up with what they need to know, so it will be impossible for librarians to be at the front of the curve on all systems needed to make users self-sufficient.

User self-sufficiency is a grand, overarching goal to stretch us and our imagination. In Browning's words, "A man's reach must exceed his grasp, or what's a heaven for?"

THE SELF-SUFFICIENT USER

What is user self-sufficiency?
Users who are self-sufficient:

> must be able to recognize when information is needed and have
> the ability to locate, evaluate, and use effectively the needed in-
> formation . . . . [they] have learned how to learn. They know
> how to learn because they know how knowledge is organized,
> how to find information, and how to use information in a way
> that others can learn from them. They are prepared for lifelong
> learning, because they can always find the information needed
> for any task or decision. (ALA Presidential Committee on Infor-
> mation Literacy 1989: 1)

Self-sufficient users:

- understand the process of acquiring current and retrospec-
  tive information and manipulate systems and services that
  locate and retrieve that information, (including an integrated set of research strategies and a knowledge of discipline-
  related tools and resources)
- evaluate the effectiveness and reliability of various information channels and sources, including libraries, for various kinds of information needs
- master specific basic skills in acquiring and storing information (e.g., faculty using databases, spreadsheets, and
  word [and information] processing packages, as well as
  books, journals, and report literature)
- recognize and articulate current and future public policy
  issues related to information (e.g., copyright, privacy, and
  privatization of government information). (Rader and
  Coons 1992: 110-111)

And finally, self-sufficient users:

- should not have to depend on a librarian to use a library
  or its resources, but only on the librarian to design and
  maintain the library so the potential of information retrieval
  remains a constant possibility.

- should be able to engage an information professional in a collaborative fashion as a resource as much as any impersonal tool. (McCrank 1992: 489)

THE EDUCATIONAL ROLE OF THE LIBRARY

If we accept the responsibility for creating self-sufficient or information-literate graduates within the context of a library organization focused on users, we have changed the frame of reference for the work of the librarian. The role of the librarian then consists of assessment, advanced information provision, resource identification and development, connection development, knowledge management, and education. All of these should be done in the context of the educational role, rather than the reference or collection development role. The education role predominates because education is the overarching library activity. Education and information literacy focus on the user and not on the librarian or the collections. Education and self-sufficiency are driven by user needs and result in a user product, not a library product. (Please note that education, not bibliographic instruction, is being used to describe what we are doing and that this is an important distinction.)

These new roles make logical the transformation of the library from a collection-centered to a user-centered structure to suit the needs and the economic environment of the twenty-first century. Instruction librarians will lead because they already have the skills and the philosophical framework to implement the new roles. For example, the knowledge gained in teaching—an understanding of information needs, user information-seeking patterns and behaviors, the organization and availability of information resources—allows librarians to help design new access tools as well as new information packaging mechanisms: a knowledge management activity. (In fact, it was instruction librarians who first identified inadequacies of collections, subject headings, and access tools for fostering diversity and proposed solutions to these deficiencies.) To truly implement viable access programs (to supplement ownership activities) in a resource identification and development role, librarians need to have a knowledge of user information needs, content, and time frames and image clarity. This knowledge comes from the systematic work with faculty to design and integrate information-seeking and use skills into the curriculum. To design effective instruction sessions and tools, assessment is critical and has been a basic activity of instruction librarians. Utilizing these skills in the broader library climate should be an easy transition for instruction librarians who are generally more library-wide and institution focused.

Connection development—going out to where the customers are rather than waiting for them to come to the library—has been expected and required of the instruction librarian to generate faculty interest in including information concepts in their courses. Advanced information provision—in-depth reference most likely provided by appointment—requires that librarians have a subject knowledge and a peer working relationship with faculty. Instruction librarians working with faculty and graduate students to develop advanced subject-intensive instructional programs and sessions have gained this kind of knowledge and generated the necessary respect to make this new activity work in the new library.

Why is the education function the key work activity/foundation for the new library and the creation of the self-sufficient user, rather than the reference function? Isn't reference the broader concept, including the education function? Certainly this argument could be made. Samuel Rothstein defines reference this way in his landmark work on the subject (1970). In fact, he defines education as the primary, or at least co-equal, function of the reference librarian, in turn supporting the contention that education is the foundation of our activities. So why not call this reference? Because the goal of reference as it is practiced today is not user self-sufficiency.

It is user dependence. It is giving information rather than making it possible for users to get information effectively on their own. It is focused on making librarians more accessible and better able to answer questions. Reference has become the reference desks, and success is having enough people there to answer every possible question. We have confused the goal—users finding/getting what they need—with the activity—staffing an on-demand desk to give users what they need. This philosophy was counter to the self-sufficiency goal and counter to the mission of the new library.

This should not be interpreted as reference bashing, but recognition of the fact that reference service must be redesigned and rethought. It must move away from a desk or place orientation and take its place as one public activity/service, not the major service activity.

It would probably be useful to explain how a user-centered library focusing on quality and education will function more effectively. You are probably asking yourself, "How can we afford to supply more classrooms or one-on-one instruction even in our new organizations?" The answer lies in how we will rethink and restructure our traditional instruction activities. With self-sufficiency as a goal, library and information systems will be made easier to use, thereby requiring less actual classroom instruction. When instruction is needed, a good deal of it will be done at the point of use and will not require human intervention (given the technology, we will not be present when most systems are used). Library signs and graphics, multimedia programs, and printed materials will readily assist users. Coursework will focus on larger issues—search strategies, information policies and economics, information organization and evaluation, etc. In-depth information consultation sessions will provide specific information needed by users. Such one-on-ones will do double duty. Librarians will be freed from housekeeping and other activities like staffing multiple service points or even much of the technical processing that now goes on. This will provide more staff to work on education and user self-sufficiency.

CONCLUSION

The upside of downsizing, if there is one, is that *in a budget crisis we can often gain support for hard choices and for radical changes that could not be made in good budget times even if they are sound and necessary changes.* Often the price of change is too high in staff discontent, faculty unrest, and administrative disapproval.

Therefore, the greatest upside to our current downsizing is that it comes at a good time. The technologies have developed to give us options, and we have organizational re-engineering models from both the public and private sectors. We have public support for radical changes. In fact, we have a mandate to make radical changes to restore confidence in our institutions. We also have the opportunity to fundamentally change libraries that have not fundamentally changed for 100 years. We can revolutionize to be more responsive to our users' needs, at the same time creating an organization that will continually change. This will eliminate our becoming frozen in the new structures and activities as we did in the old. It will mean that we will not have to have budget cuts to make the hard choices or do what we must do. Actually, if downsizing means this, maybe it's not a bad trade-off at all.

NOTES

As the role of the librarian changes, new language needs to be developed to describe that role. The terms used here are those identified for University of Arizona librarians. Assessment includes the identification of user needs as well as the evaluation of services to determine how well the library is meeting those needs in the judgment of the customers.

Advanced information provision focuses on in-depth reference by appointment as well as limited specialized reference on demand at the reference desk, via e-mail, or via phone. Resource identification and development is used to encompass collection development activities while adding on the responsibility of identifying access services and document delivery activities to meet customer needs. Connection development includes former library outreach activities, including public programming, but goes beyond those to develop connection implying two-way communication. Knowledge management involves the design of information gateways, as well as the development of new packages for information leading to better ways of creating and managing knowledge.

BIBLIOGRAPHY

Library Association Presidential Committee on Information Literacy. Final Report. Chicago: American Library Association, 1989.

McCrank, Lawrence J. "Academic Programs for Information Literacy: Theory and Structure." *RQ,* 1992; 32(4): 485-497.

Rader, Hannelore. "Bibliographic Instruction or Information Literacy." *College and Research Libraries News,* Jan. 1990; 51(1): 18-20.

Rader, Hannelore, and William Coons. "Information Literacy: One Response to the New Decades," in *The Evolving Educational Mission of the Library,* ed. by Betsy Baker and M. E. Litzinger. Chicago: Association of College and Research Libraries, 1992, pp. 109-127.

Rothstein, Samuel. *The Development of Reference Services in American Research Libraries.* Ph.D., 1954. University of Illinois, Ann Arbor, MI: University Microfilm, 1970.

2

Alternative Models for Instruction in the Academic Library: Another View of the Upside of Downsizing

Janice Simmons-Welburn
University of Iowa

The time is ripe for us to reconsider the pedagogical models we use when planning to downsize our operations. Virtually every college and university library is going through—or will go through—a period of intense reorganization in an effort to respond to an important dichotomy: We face a reduction in the power of the library budget that has been asked to do more with less, as the phrase goes—that is, to maintain collections supporting curriculum and research, pay personnel competitively, and buy and upgrade information technology while simultaneously moving toward a client-centered approach to service that is responsive to changes across the institution. We consider these issues against a backdrop of national concern for information literacy that is usually expressed outside of the library community as a desire to support independent, lifelong learning and critical thinking. A primary concern should focus upon our clientele building the necessary skills to successfully benefit from a vast array of technologies in libraries to find information, whether Opacs, CD-ROM, and multimedia workstations or end-user systems designed to access information from other sites. Several downsizing approaches, when fully developed, may contribute to the construction of post-bibliographic instructional models for the academic library of the mid-1990s. I will predicate the heart of my presentation on my views on downsizing and the conditions under which we reconsider instruction as the upside of downsizing.

DOWNSIZING

Downsizing is, in theory, working smarter, not harder—or getting the best for your dollar. We constantly hear that government and the corporate sector are high on downsizing by looking to technology for solutions to waste, inefficiency, and large and expensive workforces. More recently, the media have focused on the stress on the survivors of a downsized organization who perform and manage a broadened span of tasks and worry that one day they too will be asked to go. Management gurus such as Tom Peters call on organizations to liberate themselves from bureaucracy, fire middle management, and spur innovation in customer services.

Downsizing for any higher educational institution is, however, far more ominous. Articles published in newspapers from Philadelphia to Des Moines purport to expose the fat and waste of the university as a nonprofit organization living off the taxpayers. For the state college or university, downsizing represents a measure taken in response to deficits and reductions in funding. For the library, downsizing means recasting organizational structures and shifting personnel to better support the information needs of an increasingly diverse clientele. For the library's approach to instruction, downsizing means a reduction, if not elimination, of high cost/marginally effective approaches to teaching clientele how to get the information they need.

Downsizing may have actually contributed to an era in academic libraries best characterized as post-bibliographic instruction. I recently had the opportunity to participate in three Rethinking Reference Institutes, held at Berkeley, Duke, and, most recently, the University of Iowa. One thing is clear from group discussion in those institutes: there is no consensus on the role of instruction in client-centered services.

Dissension in our professional ranks appears to cluster around two arguments. On the one hand, our approaches to instruction, that involve teaching groups in classes and workshops, preparing detailed handouts, and one-on-one instruction, seem inadequate in the face of increasingly impatient and technologically sophisticated information seekers. On the other hand, the need for an articulated educational role becomes more imperative as the web of print and electronic information tools is spun more densely by authors, vendors, publishers, librarians, and other information providers. If there is a consensus on post-bibliographic instruction, it lies within our need for new, revised, and emerging models that promote information literacy.

I propose that we consider post-bibliographic instruction as a pedagogy with two distinguishing characteristics. First, post-bibliographic instruction must be focused on the pragmatic concerns of the information seeker. Second, this instruction is driven and contextualized by the rapid changes in information technology. My colleague James Rettig articulated this in the proceedings of the Rethinking Reference Institutes. He cited a paper presented at another conference by hypertext theoretician Ted Nelson, in which Nelson refers to a conflict between two paradigms: a technoid vision that seems to think the more complicated the better, and a paradigm of the school teacher, in which learning is systematic and rote, and the outcome is a correct answer. (Failure in this scenario is judged by an inability to produce a correct answer.) According to Rettig, ''Nelson rightly says a plague on both these houses. He calls instead for a third paradigm which emphasizes individual freedom''—a paradigm that is enabled, to some extent, by advances in computer-based information technology.[1]

I would extend Rettig's position by arguing that library-centered instruction ought to be more than the promotion of independent information seeking, which is the educational goal of bibliographic instruction. Our goal ought to be to promote the ability of an information seeker to move about with ease and freedom without having to learn esoteric nomenclature or memorize strict formulas for finding information. An era of post-bibliographic instruction recognizes:

1. the different cultures of disciplines expressed through curriculum and research, and
2. different ways of learning and knowing.

We must also recognize that instruction cannot be predicated upon pedagogical styles that are grounded in the way traditional classrooms have been conceived.

THREE SEPARATE APPROACHES

If instruction is cognizant of the pragmatic concerns of information seekers, differences in disciplinary approaches to information, and the diversity of learning styles of our clientele, then I propose that we consider three separate approaches to post-bibliographic instruction among the many that utilize new and emerging technologies:

1. group instruction in the electronic classroom that emphasizes collaborative and experiential teaching and learning,
2. instruction at the point of need, using computer-assisted instruction, or CAI, and,
3. teaching to users at remote sites over electronic information networks.

Instruction and the Electronic Classroom

My first approach, the one closest to the tradition of bibliographic instruction, is dependent on a classroom setting for introducing and teaching how to use information resources. Virtually every campus has an electronic classroom of some kind by now.

At the University of Iowa, the University Libraries opened an interactive information learning center, called the Information Arcade, several years ago. It features a state-of-the-art electronic classroom equipped with 24 networked Macintosh workstations and clusters of independent Mac, IBM, and NeXT workstations used for developing multimedia or hypermedia and for accessing text and images stored on optical disks or made available over the Internet.

Many of our instructional activities have been shifted to the Arcade classroom. The classroom is routinely used to teach short courses introducing the Internet and Oasis (the University Libraries' online information system). We are also beginning to make the Arcade classroom available for course-related instruction, research seminars, and workshops prepared by library staff. The major advantages of the classroom include the introduction of new electronic media (such as text files), online bibliographic tools, Internet sources, and hands-on learning experience with a variety of information resources.

We are only beginning to understand the capacity of the electronic classroom—using only a fraction of its potential for teaching. Maximizing instruction in an electronic classroom requires a quantum leap in the way we understand teaching. Already, I envision remarkable changes in the way we approach instruction in the Arcade classroom during the next few years. For one, we need to reconceptualize instruction as a group activity rather than as a solitary learning experience best captured by the single teacher-group learner model of the traditional classroom. Teaching in an electronic classroom ought to facilitate collaborative and experiential learning among students, an idea promoted a decade ago in the report on higher education, Involvement in Learning. Learning as a group activity also takes full advantage of the variety of talents and skills brought to the library instruction classroom by students.

In addition, the librarian who can claim to be skilled in teaching in the electronic classroom, like her colleagues on the teaching faculty, will need to become knowledgeable about computer applications in the instructional design genre to improve the presentation of ideas and materials. Presentation and multimedia software such as Persuasion™, Hypercard™, and

Supercard™ can enhance the visual display of information, enabling students to work together at individual workstations to learn what they need to, at their own pace.

Computer-Assisted Instruction

Although computer-assisted instruction is not new, the hyper-mediated environment that emerged during the 1980s has given us a new appreciation for what we can do with CAI. We have seen numerous examples of the use of hypermedia, including earlier works by librarians such as Martin Kesselman from Rutgers and Anne Bevillacqua, formerly of New York University.[2] At the University of Iowa, we combined such advances in instructional technology to create two computer-assisted instruction programs, Library Navigator and Library Explorer.

Library Navigator, a Hypercard program, is a tour of the Main Library and its services, providing maps, hours, description of service for each unit, and a glossary of terms. Library Navigator enables library users to obtain basic information about our services and the location of resources within the Main Library independently, without seeking the assistance of library personnel. The program frees our staff from routine queries, enabling them to devote their time and attention to in-depth information encounters and providing the user access at the point of need.

The Library Explorer is now in its final stages of development. Using the book as a metaphor, Library Explorer has been designed to teach basic research skills that are common to all undergraduates. The program is composed of a table of contents, three "chapters," an index, and a glossary of terms. "Chapters" 2 and 3 of the program are intended to simulate searching the libraries' online information system and selected bibliographical CD-ROM products and including summaries and quizzes that take the various learning styles of our user population into consideration.

CAI will enable us to reach new segments of our user population who neither sign up for classes nor have opportunities for course-related instruction. While we hope that the "chapters" in Library Explorer will be used sequentially, each has been designed to be used at the point of need. Let me stress once again that we anticipate two possible outcomes:

1. multimedia features such as color graphics and quick time animation will enhance the environment for learning.
2. staff will be free to devote their energies to other instructional initiatives.

This project is unique in that it resulted from the successful, long-term partnership between the professional staff of the library and computer center, and a senior faculty member and former chair of the university's prestigious rhetoric department. It is the collaborative spirit of the group that supported the success of the project.

Networked Instruction: the Next Wave

We must acknowledge that many of our users would prefer not to leave their workstations, offices, labs, dorm rooms, or homes to do a certain amount of information seeking. Many of our users have already seized the opportunity to use the Internet for more than an e-mail system. They have found it invaluable for obtaining bibliographic information from online catalogs and databases, government documents, speeches, and other types of textual and numeric data.

We need to start thinking about an invisible user population when we evaluate and reconceptualize instruction. For instance, we might use a library gopher to advertise and, where appropriate, make instruction available. Our users may sign up for instruction and participate in electronic instruction over the Internet. Many of us already know or perhaps have participated in instruction experiments over the Internet. Again, in Iowa we also look forward to completion of a fiber-optic statewide network that will have the capacity to teach interactively in a variety of community settings. This is particularly important for us because we can teach library use to students in remote locations and work in collaboration with public school systems to offer instruction to college-bound high school students and classes planning to use research materials in our library.

CONCLUSION

I conclude with a rather lengthy quote from *The Evolving Educational Mission of the Library*, the 1992 publication of the CARL Bibliographic Instruction Section. In a discussion of the changing users of academic libraries, Lizabeth Wilson wrote:

> Over the past ten years, users of academic libraries, and in particular undergraduates, have changed significantly. Due to dramatic shifts in the nation's demographics, the undergraduate population is more pluralistic, drawing increasingly from minority groups, immigrant sectors, international students, and older learners. These users have grown up in a technologically intense environment, and their increased expectations of libraries reflect this. They are from the first generation who has lived its childhood in Toffler's electronic cottage. Students come from households that are more dynamic and heterogeneous than in earlier generations. They live in a world where information increases geometrically and no one can 'get a handle on it,' where nations are interdependent, and where accelerating change is the norm. Users no longer need to come through the library doors to search for information; they are increasingly invisible as they remotely access libraries. The student of 1990 is made from different cloth than the freshman of 1980. These changed learners pose new challenges for bibliographic instruction librarians.[3]

I have attempted, throughout the course of this paper, to address the challenge of several converging forces. Not only is our user population changing; there are other factors that are equally important to us. The economic environment is forcing us to downsize at a time when information as a commodity is becoming more expensive to access. Given the shift in our user population, scholarship is increasingly decentered, and we are recognizing diverse learning styles. Moreover we are increasingly aware that our educational role as academic librarians is even more closely associated with preparing self-directed, independent, and lifelong learners.

To some degree our teaching role is simultaneously driven by and embracing new developments in information and instructional technologies, not only to identify and retrieve information, but also to be instructed on how to effectively create strategies to seek information in its variant forms. This is why I call it post-bibliographic instruction. There is no single systematic approach to teaching and learning; so much must be considered situational. The upside of downsizing is that it forces us to cast a critical eye on everything we do.

ENDNOTES

1. James Rettig, "To BI or Not to BI? That is the Question," in *Rethinking Reference in Academic Libraries.* Ed. by Anne Grodzins Lipow. Berkeley, CA: Library Solutions Press, 1993, pp. 142-3.

2. Anne Bevillacqua, *Computer-Assisted Bibliographic Instruction.* Pierian Press, 1993.

3. Lizabeth A. Wilson, "Changing Users: Bibliographic Instruction for Whom?" in *The Evolving Educational Mission of the Library*, edited by Betsy Baker and Mary Ellen Litzinger. Chicago: American Library Association, 1992, p. 49.

3

On Beyond Bill Comma Buffalo: Maximum Value, Minimum Resources, and "Good-Enoughness"

Barbara Quint
Quint and Associates/Searcher Magazine

I was asked to discuss an excellent topic—the future. And downsizing . . . hmmh, sexy topic—sort of 90s sexy, somewhere between death and ecstasy. But when I heard I would be addressing BI librarians, I had to ask, "What are they?" "Bibliographic instruction," I was told. "You're kidding," I said. "There are still people who teach that?!"

There is a classic human flaw operating here—a sort of false modesty where anybody who doesn't know everything you know must be an idiot; where you use your own personal knowledge as the common definition of universal human knowledge, and everybody who doesn't know what you know becomes subnormal by definition. For example, how many times have you watched *Jeopardy* and found yourself yelling, "Robespierre, Robespierre, Robespierre! Are you crazy or something? Were you educated in a barn?'' You assume that if you know it, everyone must know it.

And when you've known something for so very long and when practically everybody you ever talk to or deal with has also known the same thing, it's hard to believe that there is anybody left in the world who doesn't know it. Bibliographic instruction? Who wouldn't know that? Yet, of course, biblio-graphic skills have to be taught like every other piece of knowledge, every other skill.

DOCUMENT INSTRUCTION

I know that few librarians actually work in BI anymore. Biblio-graphic instruction is a thing of the past. What they really do is DI—document instruction. No client ever really wanted to learn bibliographic instruction, anyway. What they wanted was a document. Librarians just made them learn this stuff in order to find it and wouldn't give the document to them unless they learned their lesson right. Right? The only guy who really ever got excited by bibliographic instruction was Gene Garfield (founder of the Institute for Scientific Information and Science Citation Index), and he has retired. Outside of Gene, BI is ''Dead Fred'' without document delivery. So now former BI librarians have become DI librarians—drill instructors for the future, telling people how to get documents now.

Let's work through your current batting order of priorities— what you operate with today. Naturally, you define your pri-orities in a cross-relationship between availability and value. Your criteria are the right price, the right material, and the right speed of delivery.

The *first priority* for instruction obviously becomes your own online public access catalogs—OPACS—since they convey a library collection that is totally available, and usually at a rela-tively low cost to the client since the OPAC lists material al-ready acquired. *Second*, for all bibliographic citations to periodicals we naturally turn first to the CARL UnCover data-base, available free on the Internet with full document deliv-ery (though that is not free).

UnCover gives the Internet world access to over five million references. It also scares the heck out of the Information Access Company and the Institute for Scientific Information and other high-priced commercial vendors of bibliographic citations. The last time I looked up an article I wrote myself—AU = QUINT B ANDJN = ONLINE AND some title words on Social SCISearch (Social Science Citation Index)—the commercial vendors presented me with a bill for $2.50. For a citation? Where's the article? For $2.50, I want the article too! Well, CARL Un-Cover has changed the rules of the game. It has even stimulated OCLC into more aggressive competitive strategies. In this observer's opinion, OCLC would not be changing so rapidly or pricing where it is pricing if it were not for CARL.

The *third priority* should be full text sources. Naturally you don't want to waste customers' time or library staff time. Since clients want documents, give them full text. Any electronic document will instantly convert into any other form of document. Electronic documents are like air. They will fill any container. You want a fax document? Just push the button and it will sail out over a fax modem. If you don't have a fax modem, just load the ASCII file onto CompuServe or MCI Mail, and it will be transmitted as a fax document. Or you might just want to distribute it as an E-mail message over these services or over the Internet. If needed, send the document to a laser printer for a paper version. If the document arrived as an image file over a fax modem, the laser printer version may look better than the original document.

In the area of full-text document sources, you have two choices. One, of course, is the Internet. You may ask, ''Why the Internet first?'' First, because the Internet constitutes the primary—often the only—place for electronic monographs. It definitely dominates in that area. You can also get cheap monographs on some popular CD-ROMs, but how many times can you read *Aesop's Fables*? The second source is commercial online, but now we're talking real money. However, commercial dial-up services offer broad, universal coverage of periodicals, newswires, newspapers, etc. It can also handle multiple output formats (electronic, print, fax, etc.). As for value, don't forget—particularly because of their cheapness—commercial consumer utilities like Prodigy, America Online, etc. They offer some relatively unique features and great prices. Also, look into "faxback" services. Lots of newspapers run "faxback" services now.

At this point, we begin to drop below the line of top-quality, high-customer-satisfaction document instruction. You might even eliminate DI below this level, but it probably has to be included no matter how dismal. Let's talk about abstract services. Abstracts become most valuable when they substitute for documents. For example, sometimes you have clients searching for medical information who find lots of chunky abstracts on Medline. An expert may actually not need to read articles for some problems if they have a collection of really substantive abstracts. But gimpy little reading recommendations won't do the job. You need substantive content abstracts, not lightweight indicative ones. Remember, at this level, you really hope to use abstracts as document substitutes.

Even lower on the food chain, we come to online indexes. Frankly, if they're not CARL UnCover or an OPAC, they're probably not priced right for your customers. Commercial online indexes cost too much for most customers, unless they can promise document delivery in some form.

Lowest on the food chain, absolute bottom, are print indexes. History forces us to cover them because online electronic documentation sort of peters out for anything before 1972. However, print indexes as information tools for clients are pitiful, just pitiful. To maintain your professional reputation with clients, you don't want to get tarred with the same brush. Teach using printed indexes in a Don't-Let-This-Happen-To-You way, with a mutual groan. ("Aren't they ghastly?" "I know, I know. But what are we going to do?")

How do you manage document instruction? What is your goal? First, make sure that any instruction regarding library systems, particularly OPACS, is quick and easy and, preferably, *not* done by you. Everyone's favorite currency is Other People's Money; everyone's favorite resources are Other People's Time and Other People's Talent. If someone has developed a library system and sold it to your library for a lot of money, the very least they can do is take care of the instructional element. Library system instruction is a vendor negotiation issue, not a task for librarians. Your library did not hire you to do free work for vendors. You're doing them a favor just by posting notices of where the classes meet or the Internet route in use for their instruction. (Speaking of negotiating with vendors, always start high and hard: "Are you speaking to me? I am supposed to instruct people on your system?" This will be followed by widespread laughter.)

The next area is teaching the Internet, and it is really difficult. Your main excuse to your bosses for not showing up at work today is that you have to learn the Internet, and it is a grim task. The Internet is not a moving target; it is a moving ocean with you lashed to the outermost pillar of the pier watching the tide come in. Learning the Internet is like learning to breathe underwater—very, very tough without the right equipment or a lot of natural talent. You may have to perform this task yourself, without the aid of vendors.

Key online commercial vendors are the next area. Here you need customization for the data your own users need from the commercial services. Your key online services are full-text services. If a service doesn't carry a lot of full text, it definitely drops to the bottom of the list of what your clients should learn and what you want to teach. Look to full-text carriers like Dialog, Mead Data Central, Dow Jones, NewsNet, and DataStar. You also want to teach systems that can be easy to learn, remember, and use.

Quint's Law of End-User Training is quite clear on this point. If vendors haven't got the package right and the price right, don't train. You get one shot with end-users. They all have other lives to live. They are not in the library business and do not plan to spend the rest of their life learning, unlearning, and relearning systems. If the software interface is not ready, no matter how good the data or how good the price, just put it away and wait until it is ready. This holds true particularly if you come from an academic or public library with an educational role. Why train somebody to use some ghastly software—which will have to be changed or the outfit will never succeed in the end-user market anyway? Who's kidding whom? Remember, before you reject them, be sure to tell them why,

preferably in large meetings or with long letters with many sig-
natures.

Don't feel guilty when you deal aggressively with vendors.
It's for their own good. I remember what a former Vice-Presi-
dent of Meckler, Jean Paul Emard, told me once. He had gotten a call from an angry advertiser about something I had written. He gave the standard answer: "Send her a letter. She'll
publish it." The guy grumbled, "I can't." Jean Paul said, "Why
not?" "'Cause she's right!" the guy snapped back. So, you
know, it's okay when you do it for their own good. By the way,
to this list of general vendors we should also add SilverPlatter, CD-Plus, and other big online CD-ROM houses. I consider
CD-ROM to be online, just a short line.

Then comes the pit of print. What a terrible training model
it is, though. Indexers don't even go back and re-index the references that led to the introduction of new terms in the first place.
Do you know why OCLC really sprang into existence? So
catalogers could avoid the humiliation of finding copies of books
that had missed the copy-checking process and ended up classified under more than one subject classification.

Most thesauri for indexes or abstracting services (like the
Thesaurus of ERIC Descriptors) are more like suggestion lists for
free-text search strategies online. Free-text searching works better. Train users to think in terms of free-text terms, Boolean
and phrase operators, field structure, and synonyms. These are
the bibliographic document instructions you want to teach, not
Loony Toon suppositions that indexers are always ahead of the
game, always thinking up phrases that will immediately occur
to every potential user, and never, ever miscategorize anything.

To teach document instruction, take a standard online
record, show the wonders of online searching even on the short-
lined CD-ROMs, and then use Magic Markers to tag the filing
points that print indexes would have offered. Then show students how disastrously diminished retrieval would become if
limited to only the colored areas. See the little teensy pieces
of color on this massive array of machine-locatable data. Com-
pliment yourself on how you protected them from those limitations by teaching them online from the beginning. That's what

I mean by a Don't-Let-This-Happen-To-You teaching style for print instruction. However, you must also teach clients that when information has to be found, and printed tools are the only way to find it, you use them, no matter how difficult.

The most important and hardest thing to teach people is critical judgment; that even if a source is easy to use, if it's just not true or not relevant, you shouldn't use it. No matter how grisly a print source may be to use, if it happens to index the material you want covered or cover the needed date, then it is the better source. That's a pretty nasty message, so give them some sweet before you give them the sour.

MANAGING FOR A BETTER FUTURE

Since everyone is already at the document instruction stage—right?—what about that future I promised to discuss? Downsizing is the term, but what does it mean? More tasks than time is what it means, and probably more tasks than talent. So what principles do we apply under such conditions? *Principle one: no wasted motion.* Never do anything that has already been done. Swing as wide a loop as possible. If the answer lies in a vendor's drawer or in an out-of-state university's training software, find the answer and use it. Don't reinvent anything. If you find yourself having to do original, value-added work, make sure it gets maximum distribution. Give back to the support system that has given to you. Pass your improvements or experience around so no one else has to do it over.

The *second principle* is one I call *Gutgenugkeit.* After World War II the occupational forces in Germany had to help the Germans rebuild everything. The Germans, not entirely complimentary, quickly realized the difference between themselves and Americans. Germans wanted things done correctly, completely—finished, good products. But the Americans knew only two words of German when it came to quality control: ''Gut genug,'' which is German for ''good enough.'' Of course, with a country lying in ruins, a fast-moving, pragmatic strategy won. So the Germans learned to live with *Gutgenugkeit*—good-enoughness.

And that's what you have to do. Perfection is not a realistic goal. The day they downsized your staff, cut back your budget, walked off with your VCR, that was the day perfection stopped being a target. Now you must look for something with maximum value and minimum resource, something *Gutgenug.*

Principle number three. You must *define value in customer terms* as honorable, professional librarians. Value to the customer is your ethical obligation, and that includes not wasting the customer's time. What I am about to say may sound cruel, but document or bibliographic instruction is not some sort of love test. You do not get people to come to classes to prove they love you or have the proper level of respect for you and your institution. That has nothing to do with it.

The object of your performance is to get individuals the information they need and the skills they need to find more information for the rest of their lives. If that object is achieved without your ever seeing their faces as long as you live, that is fine. Frankly, the best operation would expect to never see clients. There are always more people who have not taken the class than have taken it. If you can instruct people who don't show up successfully, you probably have a better program, certainly a more flexible program, maybe even a program you can sell. Self-instructional systems or programs meet the educational goal best.

If, or when, you do use a classroom technique, be sure to start it off right. Look them dead in the eye and tell them: "This is the single most important learning experience you are going to have in your entire university career (or your entire history as a public library user). Nothing is more important than what I am about to teach you. We have all heard the story of the genie offering three wishes. Everybody knows that the smart thing to do is to ask for more wishes. This is Wish Central. I am now about to teach you how to learn about anything you will ever want to know for the rest of your lives or anything any of your friends wants to know that you don't mind trying to find for them. I am about to teach you the essence of education, which has been defined as what you remember after you've forgotten everything you learned. When you finish this class, you will be educated because this class will teach you where to find whatever information you may need for the rest of your life.''

Such a class with such an introduction must teach the most current and most futuristic technologies. The main goal of the class is not just to eliminate bother for your reference librarians or even to instruct them on how to use your library. The goal is to train them for a lifetime of learning, and since those lives will be spent in the future, future technologies are the only ones to teach. No wasted motion means no waste of customer motions.

To recap your learning order using all these principles, prioritize your own library systems. Now, does this flout our rule? Do we really choose library systems because the libraries employ us and advertise the collections because the libraries pay our salaries? No, that's not the reason. You teach library systems first and foremost because that way customers learn where to find the librarians for the rest of their lives. Libraries are where librarians work—at least for now. Teach customers to find librarians because librarians will be the friends of their mind, their protectors and teachers forevermore. Teach them how to get back to their teachers.

For library system training, rely on your library utility or vendor for basic skills, preferably using systems that require minimum hand-holding. Why? For one thing, if you want to leave a strong impression of the sophistication and dedication of librarians, you don't want to stand around teaching last name first, first name last. It's too drab and too ''Marion, Madame Librarian.'' Let a video teach such basics or some computer-assisted something. However, you do want basic skill training systems to report back. Have your system set up to report to vendors on needed improvements—computer compensations for human ignorance or indifference. For example, what about that last name first, first name last routine? Tell your vendors that's not acceptable; you'd like a Near operator instead of an Adjacency or word order operator, please. If they want concrete examples of how troublesome such rigidity becomes, what about Chinese names?

If vendors start to get argumentative, look them dead in the eye and say, ''Bill Comma Buffalo.'' Yes, that is an authorized AACR2 listing for William F. Cody—Bill Comma Buffalo. It's the truth. I can just see how it happened. Somewhere in the Azores, where the Anglo-American Cataloging Rules people must meet (between the two continents), all the catalogers with the tie-dyed shirts arguing for Buffalo Bill as the people's choice and all the people with the three-piece dress-for-success suits voting Cody Comma William F. After a long day arguing, night falls and the two groups encounter each other at a local bodega. Soon they pull their tables together and start drinking out of goatskins and singing the Melvyl Dewey theme song. Caught up in a collegial cataloging spirit, up comes the consensus vote for Bill Comma Buffalo. Now no user can find it. Users have just been sacrificed to cataloger collegiality.

INTERNET INSTRUCTION

Next training task: the Internet. The thing about the Internet, of course, is its universal reach. It can reach the commercial and the noncommercial. It can also reach people. There lies the next future. Someday you will finish with your task of document instruction as you have finished bibliographic instruction. The next phase is information instruction—connecting readers with authors and eliminating the middle people, such as scholarly publishers.

Today the Internet is completely out of control. So what is our principle? *Gutgenugkeit.* Good-enoughness. Establish criteria—the first being that whatever sources you teach must be stable. They must be sources that will endure, that are networked, that have gophers connected to the mother gopher in Michigan, that have clear, continuous data suppliers. You also need some guarantee of quality, someone to make sure that the data sent was the same as the data received, that passing through half a dozen hands and networks didn't alter it. You also need continuity, to know that if the supplier provides volume one, they will also supply volume two. Otherwise, it's not worth your trouble to teach it. You also need good interfaces. Again, if you have to design those interfaces, remember to share them and notify all the bulletin boards and Listservs. And never, ever design an interface before checking to see whether some other poor soul has already designed it. Even if the other interface is not perfect, you can build around it.

Full-text commercial services can cover periodicals, newspapers, and newswires well. Consumer utilities have the advantage of great prices and also graphics, but they have lousy search engines and usually very thin data with skimpy back files. Faxback is hot and hyped. Watch out for the hype. If you sell expensive intermediated searches and clients read that they could get the same thing for a dollar, off the side of a bus, it could be dangerous for professional searchers. Do the words ''professional suicide'' mean anything to you?

As for abstracts on CD-ROMs, make them self-instructional, but warn clients about what they don't contain. Help develop your clientele's critical sense. For example, next to any CD-ROM, I would put a notice about currency and missing back files available in dial-up or in print and uncovered formats like monographs in periodical abstracting sources. Maybe you could share whatever warning charts and forms you develop. Again, if someone's done it once, you don't want to do it over again— no wasted motion. Such notices also remind clients that the librarians are on top of every data source. The forms could also show print source equivalents and dial-up online equivalents, plus a list of advantages and disadvantages. Again, the posters perform an educational role with maximum efficiency. They could also serve as a marvelous discipline to vendors, pressing them to include more.

As for commercial online index databases with only bibliographic information, that's a dying area. CARL could kill them if it keeps grinding out its free UnCover references. For print index training, identify those that are not online, provide a list to clients, and offer consultation on demand. But never let them think you like it.

As for the future of information instruction, what's the most necessary, under performed task in information work today? Internet foraging. I mean people who put on their pith helmets, plop their trusty shotguns on their shoulders, lace up their boots, and head off into the bush looking for data. People who build the gophers, record the telnets, write the Internet reference books, go looking for meat.

The second, most-needed function is Internet archivists. The Internet has to be disciplined, constructed, and given standards such as a bibliographic citation system of its own. And it's our job to do it. It's also our job to pressure vendors building the scholarly megabases to adjust to the Internet reality, to at least record the Internet addresses of all their listed authors. Why not? Think what a marketing tool it would make for them.

How can you sell them on the idea? Point out that sooner or later primary scholarly publishers will hit the wall. (Splat). Sooner or later authors and readers are going to communicate directly. When publishers start charging for every reproduction of single articles, they will destroy their own subscription business. Why buy subscriptions if you have to pay for every article? Sooner or later some author who has already been stupid enough to pay page charges to provide publishers with the product they sell will end up being charged for reproducing his or her own articles. And that's when faculty will realize there's a lot of money going to people who didn't pay anything for the research. Why shouldn't the funder—the university paying salaries or the government agency or foundation supporting research projects or even the professional association—get the money instead of the commercial publisher?

Librarians need to get ready for the next phase and lead it. Remind the megabase creators that you deal directly with many of their authors. With you as a bridge, we can create a new system of scholarly communication using the authors, the access tool creators, Internet archivists, and readers.

You're all in the document delivery business now. So let's negotiate good deals. And that includes document delivery of abstracts and indexing and deals with Dialog, Mead, et al. More than 50 percent of Mead's new subscriber deals come through custom contracts. Don't be the only one in the world still paying retail. And integrate document delivery with bibliographic citations. Keep looking for the sweet deals that can merge collection and document delivery with access tools. Take advantage of the new DIALOG ERA (Electronic Redistribution and

Archiving) program. For the first time in a long time, a commercial database service has finally done something to indicate it knows where the on-ramp to the Information Superhighway is. For the first time in a long time, the industry has surprised me. The internal name for the project at DIALOG was Dam Busters. The new program substantially eliminates most of the problems in dealing with copyright, terms, and conditions barriers to re-use. You can now think of the entire Dialog system as one giant clipping file. One expects other services will follow DIALOG's lead. DIALOG ERA lets you haul off whatever you choose; not just one-time copies but network access.

Another area that needs work is categorizing sources by the capacity of your users. Editors and publishers kind of do that, but it needs more work. For example, medical data. You distribute certain kinds of medical data to certain levels of knowledge. There should be a natural building process, with people graduating from Health Periodicals Database to Medline. Help clients progress through different stages and expand their ability to absorb information. Identifying people as sources is part of that process.

One last point. I love all librarians. And I know that it is a lot easier to talk the talk than to walk the walk. I know it is going to take time and trouble and talent to put it all together. But I'll tell you something about talking and walking: The longest and weariest walk you will ever take in your life is the walk back from heading in the wrong direction.

4

Overcoming Mazes and Minotaurs: Achieving User Independence in the Academic Library Labyrinth

Dr. Ann Coder and Margie Smith
University of Hawaii

THE NATURE OF THE PROBLEM

The young Athenian men and women sent to Crete to be offered to the Minotaur might be said to resemble our young women and men sent off to the university library. They too face the task of trying to survive in a labyrinthine environment.

Unlike the stable stone walls of the labyrinth in Minos, the information environment our library users confront is more akin to Mark Twain's experience as a Mississippi river pilot, where each trip down the river of information brings a shift of channels. New electronic databases, changes in the software of existing databases, context-driven option lines within a database, and function keys meaning different things in different databases confront the library user at every turn.

The response of librarians has conventionally been to work harder to answer more user questions, teach more BI classes, attempt to reach every freshman English class, or work to introduce a required library skills course into the college curriculum.

Despite trying harder and doing more, we simply fell further behind. At times reference librarians began to feel like minotaurs themselves as staff coped with an increasing volume of repetitive questions. Because there was insufficient time to perform up to their high public service standards, staff experienced mounting stress and frustration. Librarians' discussions occasionally degenerated into blaming the students for asking the same ''dumb'' questions and musing about whether the students were college material.

But librarians have come to empathize with users as we attempt to master new information sources such as the Internet. We too are searching for patterns, organization, coherence, comprehensibility, and stability. Both librarians and users are now immersed in the Great Information Flood, and the rivers have overflowed their banks. Unable to stop the rain of information, we have begun to look for new ways to help people stay afloat.

Previously we were so busy rescuing people downriver that no one was dispatched to investigate why users were falling in upstream. Although for years the reference staff had observed that certain questions were asked over and over, it took the impact of the new information reality to motivate librarians to begin analyzing the types of questions and problems common to many library users.

In reviewing the situation, we saw that the library had an abundance of signs attempting to convey information. However, the conventional wisdom that people don't read signs seemed to be correct. As we looked more closely at this situation, we realized that there was little sense of coherence in the signs. There was no attempt to present an overall picture of how the library, and the information it contained, was organized. In short, we had not analyzed our problems from an information systems point of view that included the users.

Aaron Antonovsky provides a helpful systems theory and information processing framework. The individual is seen as a system:

1. linked to/isolated from suprasystems, from which
2. information/noise is received;
3. these messages are then internally integrated/deciphered by the system, which then
4. sends information/noise to the suprasystems, which
5. provide feedback/ignore the messages. (Antonovsky, 1993, p. 970)

Looking at this cycle in terms of the library user/library,

1. the user comes into the library isolated from an understanding of the library's internal information structures;
2. the information the library provides is thus received as noise; and
3. the user is therefore unable to decipher the information, so
4. the user then asks questions of the librarians, and
5. the librarians provide feedback to the individual questions but ignore the meaning behind all of these messages, i.e., that the library is failing to provide a comprehensive overview.

Again, to quote Antonovsky:

Information theory perhaps expresses it best of all: The more complex the messages directed at a person, the greater the potential for noise rather than information; the greater the difficulty in integrating the information in the internal processing system; the greater the danger of confusion of output. (Ibid.)

It became clear that we needed to rethink our library signage system in order to convey to the users the underlying organizational principles of the library. The underlying goal of this project was to enable an intelligent human being to come into the library and, with only the assistance of the point-of-use displays, successfully navigate the library.

However, our goal was not simply intellectual. We also wanted the users to feel that the library is not a labyrinth designed deliberately to confuse them. We wanted the information we would provide to be a statement about the library's desire to make itself comprehensible to its users. The affective component of the message is particularly important given the recent findings that people's confidence in using a library empowers them to tackle new challenges more successfully. (Nahl, 1993, pp. 160-164, 212)

We soon realized that the library's complexities were invisible to staff who had worked there for a number of years. Therefore we began to analyze users' problems by debriefing new librarians and library school student interns, whose perspective was similar to that of incoming students in general. Their insights helped create an awareness of the library's difficulties as experienced by the user. We read the response papers written by graduate library school students after their first semester, tabulated information desk questions by category, and analyzed users' comments on the suggestion board in an ongoing cycle of analysis and response.

Once we had a sense of the most common problems, we began to consider point-of-use displays as an additional instructional approach. If BI can be equated with driver education, what we attempted was to develop a program of AAA trip planning and roadside assistance, including road maps and signs.

DESIGN PRINCIPLES

Several graphic and design principles emerged from our experiences in creating point-of-use instructional materials. These may be summarized as Clarify, Simplify, Locate, and Enlarge.

Clarify

By "clarify," we mean that librarians must determine exactly what patrons need to know at any given point. Many librarians either assume that users know as much about libraries as librarians know or that they ought to. Others succumb to the temptation to turn patrons into mini-librarians by telling them everything all at once.

Library self-instructional displays often miss the step of clarifying exactly how much users need to know and can become floodplains of information, a meaningless jumble of excess. To introduce users to an alien structure, information must be pared down to the barest essentials, so as not to overwhelm them. What is needed are signs that are an aid to cognitive mapping—devices for assisting users to see a pattern, and the underlying organizational structures of the library. Edward Tufte summed this up very well: Confusion and clutter are failures of design, not attributes of information. And so the point is to find design strategies that reveal detail and complexity—rather than to fault the data for an excess of complication. Or, worse, to fault viewers for a lack of understanding (Tufte, 1990, p. 53).

One of the problems inherent in using the library is assuming that users are familiar with library terminology. Terms such as OPAC, PAC, CD-ROMs, etc., are so common in library parlance that they are almost invisible to librarians, yet they often puzzle novice users. To further confuse users, librarians often abbreviate phrases that have little meaning to the public in the first place.

Realizing that it was not important for users to understand what the term PAC meant, we made signs that instead referred to the "computerized catalog." A study done by Rachael Naismith and Joan Stein at Carnegie Mellon University found that the average student understood only half of the common library jargon, such as "command search," "multivolume set," and "nonprint materials" (1989, p. 549). One student said that a "citation is like a ticket or something for speeding" (1989, p. 551).

Simplify

Menin and Benning (1992) emphasize about point-of-purchase (P.O.P.) advertising that,

> Everything you put into the store must be able to do its job in the split second it catches the consumer's eye. The message need not necessarily be written. It can be conveyed by pictures, graphics, and theme subjects. In fact, the fewer words in P.O.P., the faster the communication (p. 53).

Tufte expresses the same idea with "Every bit of ink on a graphic requires a reason. And nearly always that reason should be that the ink presents new information" (1983, p. 96).

Visual icons and symbols for words were substituted wherever possible in the point-of-use self-instructional displays, somewhat akin to the highway symbols used instead of words for "no left turn." Because pictures engage a different cognitive mode of interacting with the environment, by combining pictures with words, the number of channels available for communication was doubled. Also, because pictures are more concrete than words, their content can be absorbed more easily. Tufte (1990) says that "to envision information . . . is to work at the intersection of image, word, number, art" (p. 9).

Zipf (1965, p. 5) points out that people tend to do what requires the least effort. Thus, the simplification of signs, the reduction of the content to the barest essentials, appeals to the user as the fastest and easiest way of obtaining information. The maxim of limiting posters to seven words is a guiding principle, although this principle is often violated in practice.

This might be envisioned as the Big Mac or fast-food model. As soon as one enters a fast-food restaurant, one sees pictures of what is available to order and has an immediate understanding of where to stand in line. Contrast this with the elegant continental restaurant, dimly lit, with its menu in French. Kinsey Millhone, in Sue Grafton's *G is for Gumshoe*, describes her experience at an expensive hotel restaurant:

> I'm used to fast food chains where the menus feature glossy photos of the food. . . . The edibles here were itemized on a quarto of parchment, handwrit by some kitchen scribe who had mastered Foodspeak. " . . . lightly sauced pan-smoked filets of free range veal in a crib of fresh phyllo, topped with squaw bush berries, and accompanied by hand-formed gaufrettes of goat cheese, wild mushrooms, yampa root, and fresh herbs . . . " $21.95 . . . As usual, I could tell I was completely out of my element. I hardly ever eat squaw bush berries and yampa root. . . . (1990, pp. 150-151)

The fast-food restaurant exudes an atmosphere of friendly assurance and intelligibility. The fine dining experience makes the uninitiated feel slightly ill at ease.

Locate

A third principle we considered was location. Four aspects of location were reviewed:

- eye level
- alignment of maps
- traffic patterns
- placing the answer where the question is asked

Eye level: The tasteful, commercially produced building signs installed when the University of Hawaii's Library was constructed were placed either below or above eye level. This provided an excellent example of what not to emulate and reinforced the common conception that no one read signs anyway. In contrast, the new instructional signs were placed at eye level and in high-traffic locations, where they could be easily seen. The ADA regulations acknowledge the importance of the concept of eye-level positioning.

Alignment: One often-overlooked aspect of positioning a map is to align it with what it represents. As Levine, Marchon, and Hanley (1984, p. 149) point out, people ignore the "you are here" arrow and assume that items higher up on the map are always forward in the terrain (aligned). When a map is "contra-aligned," most people interpret the information as if the map were aligned—that is, incorrectly (Levine, Marchon and Hanley, p. 151).

Traffic patterns are another important consideration in selecting a location. We put an information kiosk in the entrance lobby, where everyone entering the library would be sure to see it. Its purpose was to make users feel welcome and to assist them in understanding the library's basic organizing principles.

Placing the answer where the question is asked: The kiosk contained information a person just entering the building would want to know, based on an analysis of questions most commonly asked at the nearby information desk.

One panel says "Welcome to Hamilton Library" and includes a map of the first floor, with the locations of the major collections. Another panel, entitled "How to find a book," shows how to search the online catalog at the adjacent terminals and gives call number locations for users who have just completed their catalog search. There is also a panel containing a large library directory for those who already know where they want to go.

Between the entrance and the information kiosk are two high tables with a selection of self-instructional handouts: a self-guided library tour, a floor plan, a page on using the computerized catalog, etc. These are intended to provide more detailed information than is appropriate for the kiosk and can be taken and used in other locations. These handouts were initially in a vertical rack next to the kiosk, but when they were placed on tables, in individual trays with legible labels at eye level, and moved closer to the entrance, the number taken increased dramatically.

Since one of the important aspects of location is to place information where it needs to be known and used, a detailed map of all floors of the library would be too much information for the users at the entrance. They would not remember it later and do not yet know where they need to go. Hence, a floor plan of the building that they can take with them is more effective than a large-scale, stationary map. Information kiosks across from each of the second floor elevator banks have detailed second-floor plans.

The second floor kiosk at the entrance to the stacks was also used to respond to another problem. The circulation staff had found that almost a third of the books they were asked to search for were in their proper place on the shelves. This indicated that many of our users were unable to find books even when they had the correct call number. We created a panel telling users how to read a call number. We highlighted the fact that Cutter numbers are decimal numbers—a major obstacle to finding books.

ENLARGE

Signs must be visible from a distance, especially to attract the attention of users who do not even realize that they should have a question or need information. By their size alone, large signs present a strong nonverbal clue that they contain information users need to know. There is also the strong, if implicit, message that the library does not consider this information to be self-evident and that the library wants the user to know this information.

Some of these displays are on a scale that graphics principles say could be seen from the nearest freeway at a speed of 60 miles per hour. Some library staff have jokingly dubbed these extra-large displays ''trained attack signs.'' This ridicule is a small price to pay for the benefits of replacing small and tasteful with effective and eye-catching.

We used enlargement to respond to a common problem: after finishing a CD-ROM search, users were constantly asking us how to find journal articles. We did have copies of the printed serials list lying about, but their covers had a small, wordy label that was only 2.5 by 4 inches. Those labels were replaced by 6-by-12-inch labels saying ''Journal List'' in two-inch-high letters. That enlargement, coupled with a copy displayed prominently on a dictionary stand beside the reference desk, with a 30-inch-high standing sign saying ''Journal List,'' made it much easier for library users to answer their own question about the next step in their research process.

TECHNICAL ASPECTS

Our first large-scale plunge into point-of-use self-instructional displays came in December 1990, when we changed software vendors and created a set of panels totaling 36 square feet that described how to search the newly installed online catalog. This display was hung on the windows at our entrance. It was well received and led us to realize the potential of the Macintosh/laser printer combination. In the past our choice had been between quick homemade, hand-lettered signs and slow, expensive, but attractive commercially–produced signs. Now, with the Macintosh/laser printer combination, we could produce quick, inexpensive displays with a professional look.

For years our reference department had talked longingly about having an information kiosk in the lobby to help orient users to the library, but we were deterred by the expense. The

Macintosh and the laser printer liberated us from reliance upon expensive, commercially–produced signage, and we were able to look again at the idea of a kiosk. We had found a way to produce the displays; we just needed something to put them on. Over a coffee break, the idea of using hollow-core, unfinished interior doors came to us. They could be hinged together, painted, and strutted at the top for stability. And they would be cheap!

Feeling like bibliographic guerrillas, we set out to take back the library for the users, freeing them from rigid and unchangeable commercial signage. Due to the success of our window display, we were able to secure administrative support and soon had a purchase order for $200 to buy six doors, paint, and hinges.

We used the enlarge feature on the laser printer, ran off the design, trimmed the margins on two of the four sides of each 8 1/2-by-11-inch sheet, overlapped and rubber cemented the margins on the other two sides, rubber cemented them to a support paper, laminated them to protect them from graffiti, and hung them on the wooden panels/doors.

One thing we discovered was that, unlike expensive commercially–produced signs, we were able to show a small version of the actual finished product to our colleagues for comments and critique. This allowed us to go through several iterations before committing ourselves to the work of creating a large-scale version. Changes were quite easy in the scale model but were also feasible in the large scale. Thus, it was an ideal medium for signage in an environment of continuous change.

Expanding beyond the kiosk, we began to look at other locations in the library where questions arose and needed to be answered. This led us to the use of colored and white plastic boards (Sintra boards) as reusable background material on which to mount the signs. With the plastic boards we had the support, frame, and contrasting border all at the same time.

We soon discovered that we did not need to laminate the displays. A pilot mock-up on the second floor that we hadn't laminated because of its projected short-term life ended up staying for almost a year with no damage. This allowed us to create all subsequent displays more easily because we didn't have to laminate them.

We took this lack of graffiti as a positive sign that our users recognized our good intentions and that our goal of empowering them to navigate the Library labyrinth successfully had been at least partially met. Our display panels, while still in a continuous cycle of improvement, were conveying the effective message that the library was not run by Minotaurs, but by librarians who care about helping people find their way within today's complex information structure.

BIBLIOGRAPHY

Antonovsky, A. (1993) "Complexity, Conflict, Chaos, Coherence, Coercion and Civility." *Social Sciences and Medicine*, 38 (8), 1993. p. 970.

Grafton, S. (1990) *"G" Is for Gumshoe.* New York: Fawcett Crest. pp. 150-151.

Levine, M., I. Marchon, and G. Hanley (1984) "The Placement and Misplacement of You-Are-Here Maps." *Environment and Behavior*, 16(2). pp. 149,151.

Menin, B. and A. E. Benning Sr. (1992) *The Power of Point-of-Purchase Advertising.* New York: AMACOM. p. 53.

Nahl, D. (1993) "CD-ROM Point-of-Use Instructions for Novice Searchers: A Comparison of User-Centered Affectively Elaborated and System-Centered Unelaborated Text." University of Hawaii Ph.D. dissertation.

Naismith, R., and J. Stein (1989) "Library Jargon: Student Comprehension of Technical Language Used by Librarians." *College and Research Libraries*, 50(5).

Tufte, E. (1990) *Envisioning Information.* Cheshire, CT: Graphics Press.

Tufte, E. (1983) *The Visual Display of Quantitative Information.* Cheshire, CT: Graphics Press.

Zipf, G. K. (1965) *Human Behavior and the Principle of Least Effort: An Introduction to Human Ecology.* New York: Hafner Publishing Company.

5

Public Service Strategies for Minimizing Library Anxiety

Sherry DeDecker with Lynn Westbrook
University of California at Santa Barbara/
University of Michigan

Academic public service librarians face many challenges and opportunities in guiding users through the information jungle. While managing significant budget cuts, we often protect our core services: instruction and reference. In order to maximize the effectiveness of those services, we must present them in an atmosphere that encourages users to come to us for assistance.

Library anxiety, as described by Constance Mellon, often undermines our work. She identified four causes of student fear in the academic library:

1. the size of the library,
2. a lack of knowledge about where to go,
3. how to begin, and
4. what to do (Mellon, 162).

Other ideas have augmented her work, such as Stebelman's comment that the "current transitional stage" of library technology means that the "predictability of libraries has significantly decreased" (Bungard, 146). Kuhlthau identifies anxiety as an integral part of the research process, a natural state that will be lessened as the user is brought to an understanding of the dynamics of the information search process as a whole (Kuhlthau, 1993, p. 8).

Many ideas have been presented for dealing with specific aspects of this barrier which prevents competent library use. However, it seems that instead of the problem being alleviated, it is growing worse. The combination of exponential information growth and deep cuts in higher education funding is creating a situation in which single, limited responses are ineffective. In addition to users being exposed to traditional sources, they now face the ever-increasing plethora of electronic sources that change faster than they can be assimilated. In addition, these tools are not standardized and offer varying degrees of user-friendliness. Messages range from "your search term is not in our catalog" to "0 results; consider changing your search strategy." Users may well hesitate to ask for help at a reference desk, simply because they don't know how to formulate the question. Rather than handle these complexities, they retreat from the library.

What a shame, when we have so many great sources for them to use to expand their research opportunities! At least five barriers come between users and a committed public service staff. First, many first-year students are unprepared for an electronic information environment. According to the Digest of Education Statistics, as of 1989, computer use in high schools was at 39.2 percent. Even assuming that this percentage will increase as more secondary schools become computerized, we can expect that fully half our high school students may be unfamiliar with computers or have limited knowledge of them. Also, although home computers are becoming more popular, only 20.7 percent of high school students use them (Digest of Education Statistics, p. 435).

Second, the increasing diversity of the student population is reflected in students' needs and information perspectives.

Students bring to the library expectations they have learned in different settings. They may come from a suburban high school with adequate resources or from a large urban high school that has been beset with budget cuts. They may come from another country, where the libraries operate with closed stacks. They may be returning to the academic setting as adult learners. They may have disabilities and require special services to enable them to access resources. They may be first-generation college students who do not have the advantage of a family mentor to advise them. In addition, the increasing ethnic and racial diversity of today's student body means that monolithic library settings match the experiences of fewer students.

Third, the information explosion is a reality for both users and librarians. That reality and the perception of its impact are problematic. It is difficult for librarians to keep up with the vast array of sources made available today; think of how much more impossible it must seem for students.

Fourth, we must not overlook the effect library downsizing has had on services. Fewer librarians are available for service at a time when more service is needed. At UCSB, for example, we have merged our social sciences and humanities reference desk with government publications reference. It will take time for us to assimilate the new knowledge in order to provide effective service to our clientele. The loss of valued support staff and basic equipment funding contribute to the pressure.

Finally, there is that familiar student phenomenon, fear of the unknown. Academic libraries have always appeared intimidating to many students and are even more so now, with a daunting array of information sources: Some libraries still use the card catalog, while others are online; some are using paper indexes, while others have moved into CDs or online databases (or combinations, all with different search strategies). Given all these formats, there is no reason to believe students are becoming more comfortable in our libraries.

With such barriers to effective library use during this period of downsizing, what principles serve to guide librarians in their efforts to minimize library anxiety? In general, as many have done for the past two decades, we must understand the elements of learning theory that most inform our work with students.

Carol Kuhlthau's new book provides an excellent overview of the most pertinent learning theory. She notes, "The constructivist view of learning, which offers insight into what the user experiences, is a particularly valuable way to understand information seeking from the user's perspective. Two basic themes run through the theory of construction. One is that we construct our own unique personal worlds, and the other is that construction involves the total person incorporating thinking, feeling, and acting in a dynamic process of learning" (Kuhlthau, 1993).

Every aspect of public services can reflect an understanding of these themes. As suggested by that first theme, instead of thinking of the library as a collection of physical entities and services that are presented to patrons, visualize the library as patrons experience it. That is how they construct meaning from our actions, signs, and so on. If we understand the library from the perspective of the patron, then we have new power over how we help a patron learn to use it. As suggested by that second theme, instead of thinking of patron activities as simple, goal-driven encounters with the library, visualize each step as a part of a dynamic learning process that involves emotions as well as actions and thought. If we understand patron activities from that perspective, then we have a greater range of teaching opportunities.

Kuhlthau has built on Belkin's anomalous states of knowledge (ASK) and Taylor's four levels of the information process to create her own six-stage model of the process. She acknowledged the value of Taylor's four levels:

1. the visceral level, in which a need is actual but unexpressed;
2. the conscious level, in which an internal description is formed;
3. the formalized level, in which a formal statement is made;
4. the compromised level, which is the question as it is presented to an information system.

Relating these levels to Belkin's theory, "the user's ability to articulate requests to the information system can be expected to change according to his or her level of understanding of the problem (Kuhlthau, 1991).

Considering the affective components of the learning process has become increasingly crucial. As Corno and Kanfer note, recognizing that they have some degree of control over a difficult learning task can help people maintain the drive needed to complete it. "When tasks must be completed in the face of difficulties, aspects of cognition, motivation, and emotion require specialized control. The sense that one can control these inner states, coupled with an understanding of the nature of such mechanisms, contributes momentum toward goal attainment" (Corno and Kanfer, p. 303).

Finally, given various opportunities for interaction with patrons, an understanding of personal learning styles can enhance those contacts made with individuals and small groups. Kolb's identification of four primary learning styles continues to be developed and explored by scholars in many fields. Kolb, whose ideas are well summarized by Green et al., identified divergers, assimilators, convergers, and accommodaters (Green, Snell, and Parimanath, 1990). All have their strengths and weaknesses; all can be incorporated in many public service settings.

STRATEGIES: PROGRAMS THAT WORK

Given the aforementioned barriers to effective library use, it becomes necessary for public services staff to view their decisions, at least in part, through the lens of library anxiety. At planning meetings as well as in the daily management of the library, everyone can add this consideration to their list of decision criteria. When examining the entire public services effort in light of library anxiety, staff may find it useful to consider three major areas: physical invitations, staff training, and services. These areas cover virtually every patron interaction with the library.

PHYSICAL INVITATIONS

This is an area worth examining because, once set up well, it does not take much in the way of staff or resources to maintain. It also provides that important first impression your clientele will carry with them for a long time. Consider the message your library projects; Is it a friendly one? There are many ways to make it so; here a few major ones:

Signs:
Maps help users navigate the library. "Users who can thus form a mental picture of the environment will move about it with some degree of confidence" (Kupersmith, p. 37). Posted rules need to be phrased in such a way as to get the message across without imparting an unfriendly image. Consider the effect of this message, designed by Pennsylvania State Library: "RAVENOUS ROACHES RAVAGE ROOT BEER & RARE BOOKS! Don't eat or drink in the library" (Clement, 1994).

Exhibits:
Do they reflect the diversity of your user population? Are they engaging? Challenging? Affirming? Do they reflect campus interests?

Bulletin boards:
A great way to advertise library services or programs. They can also be used as a campus information resource; in addition to advertising programs throughout the campus community, they act as a magnet to draw people into the library.

Handouts:
These should be clear and should reflect only the major points of instruction. They should be carefully screened to avoid library jargon. (What is a database?) If a tool requires more detailed instruction for the more sophisticated user, consider putting advanced instructions on a second handout which uses search examples with authors and topics reflecting diverse ethnic groups. Handouts are another way to reflect multiculturalism.

Subject-specific reference guides:
These help users find the right section of the reference collection in which to begin their research. Listing the major electronic sources for each subject in these guides will at least point users in the right direction. At UCSB, we put the name, phone number, and e-mail address of the collection manager on each subject guide. We also note on all guides and handouts, ''If you need help, ask at the reference desk.''

STAFF TRAINING

This area covers everyone from students who are left at the circulation desk after all full-time staff have left the building to the newly promoted manager. Investing time and effort in staff training boosts morale, helps people to become more flexible as they all become familiar with certain basics, and can be your strongest patron link when equipment and services must be limited. When staff are not kept up to date on new resources, they are left in the unenviable position of explaining the unfamiliar to library users.

Given the rapidly changing nature of electronic sources in our libraries, preparing librarians and staff to become knowledgeable about all available finding tools can be challenging. It is helpful to have one person in charge of developing programs to assist staff in keeping up with all the changes.

Regularly scheduled training sessions are a useful way of keeping staff up-to-date. They provide an opportunity to ensure that all staff have been briefed on dealing with the public: basic phone manners, dealing with frustrated or angry patrons, helping the shy or anxious user, the importance of good referrals, etc. For librarians and staff who are more directly involved in the reference process, strategies we all know but tend to forget during crunch times can be reviewed: for example, the importance of neutral questioning and closing the reference interview with a referral or invitation to return. Training sessions are also a good way to ensure that all staff are informed of recent changes in library policy or programs on campus that will impact the library.

At UCSB, in addition to the general staff meeting, we have a training session for librarians scheduled once a month. During these sessions, librarians demonstrate new finding tools. We also use this time to provide additional instruction in each of our subject areas: the basic reference sources, common questions, etc. We set aside some time at each reference meeting for a "look at this great source I found" session.

SERVICES TO USERS

Services cover every planned interaction with patrons. Their preparation allows maximization of what has been learned in staff training, and their continuity provides an opportunity to constantly improve and adjust patron contacts. In developing this area, USCB identified types of services that seem to be particularly effective in providing a welcoming atmosphere for users.

OUTREACH

When librarians go into high schools or residence halls, visit with faculty and teaching assistants, or maintain an electronic connection to outside users, they provide a way to reach those who don't come into the library. These individuals may be potential clients who are unaware of the variety of resources available to them or high school students who represent our future users. We may be reaching beyond the library walls to our faceless clientele-those whose connection to the library consists of searching at a remote terminal. By extending ourselves in a variety of creative ways, we help potential users see the value of our services. We should take advantage of every chance we get to develop rapport with those who can serve as a resource to encourage increased library use.

Programs for high schools:
Some librarians go into local high schools to provide basic instruction to students. Handouts are used to provide a starting point for beginning research. Such instruction has been suc-

cessful at the University of Michigan as well as on other campuses (Canelas and Westbrook, 1990). Developing a link between college and high school librarians will pave the way for a smoother transition for students into the more complicated university environment.

Development of rapport with faculty:

Classes and office hours encourage students to ask librarians questions, but another successful strategy for motivating students to come to us is to develop and maintain a strong working relationship between librarians, faculty, and teaching assistants. Visiting new faculty with offers of instruction for their students will help open doors. If this is not possible due to time constraints, library staff can recruit a liaison within each department through whom they can promote services or conduct informational sessions with graduate students and encourage them to send students to the library for assistance.

Marketing library services available to faculty and students puts a more friendly face on the library and its staff. At UCSB, we send quarterly letters to faculty advertising new sources and offering instruction. We have also developed a newsletter that we send to all faculty and graduate students.

Faculty-librarian information forums also help to humanize librarians. During these forums, faculty come into the library to discuss their research interests and help us to understand which types of sources and services are most useful to them and their students.

UC Berkeley has developed faculty seminars specifically geared toward teaching use of electronic resources. These seminars are popular with faculty and graduate students alike and have proved to be an effective means of keeping faculty up-to-date on new methods of accessing material (Lipow, 1991).

Outreach to students:

Each fall, librarians and staff at the University of Michigan host an information fair, called InfoFest, with the staff of the small libraries within the residence halls. Programs such as InfoFest are a great way to reach reluctant or non-library users in their own setting. Students discover some of the services available to them and have an opportunity to meet the staff they will be encountering when they visit the library.

Electronic reference:
This refers to users receiving specific reference help from librarians for questions sent by e-mail. This concept is being implemented in a few libraries, most notably Indiana University (Bristow, 1992). A potential advantage of increased use of this type of service could be decreased telephone reference.

It is estimated that 60 percent of remote users rarely or never use MELVYL, the OPAC for the University of California, in a UC library (Millsap and Ferl, p. 323). Since these users represent one-third of MELVYL searches, it is time to consider how we can best meet the needs of this growing segment of the library user population.

PROGRAMS

By acknowledging the tremendous amount of information available today, we can help our users feel more comfortable in admitting their apprehension. "Lectures and instruction programs that let students know that everybody experiences anxiety and that asking for help is an important part of the search process can go a long way toward making students' initial library experiences less stressful" (Keefer, 337). Instruction sessions should encompass a variety of techniques designed to teach to a range of learning styles. Again, use of multicultural or varying gender themes in instruction examples is another way to help users from all walks of life feel more in touch with the academic library environment. Encouraging input from students during instruction programs will help increase interest and make these sessions more relevant to specific needs.

Term paper counseling:
Although this type of program has been in existence for years, it is worth a new look as librarians feel the pressure of instructing with fewer people to share the workload. Many librarians find this type of point-of-need instruction effective in alleviating students' anxiety when they start the research process. Northwestern University provides a good example of the success of this type of program (Sarkodie-Mensah 1989).

E-mail:

At UCSB and the University of Michigan, we now encourage students to get e-mail accounts and send us messages when they have questions about material covered during instruction sessions or when they need help with research. This type of service is a new concept for students and librarians, but, like electronic reference, it's just beginning to be used. Once they get over their initial anxiety, students seem to enjoy this connection with librarians. Coupled with an invitation to visit us personally or to phone with questions, e-mail provides another way for the hesitant student to approach us.

Electronic classrooms:

At UCSB, we opened our new electronic classroom this past fall. We have 24 terminals configured to search our two OPACs (PEGASUS, our in-house system, and MELVYL), as well as to connect to the Internet.

Students have responded positively to this hands-on type of learning. However, we have found it necessary to change our teaching styles somewhat. Due to the varying computer-experience level of students, we must go slower than before with our instruction. We have found it helpful to have the students watch us demonstrate the search first, then give them time to practice. This is an environment where team teaching is really beneficial.

Collaborative learning:

Having students use the terminals in pairs during instruction sessions seems to be more effective in easing their anxiety and frustration, especially for those new to electronic searching. An evaluation of a program at Millersville University in Pennsylvania found that most students felt pairing was beneficial to them (Warmkessel and Carothers, 1993). As libraries design programs with more emphasis on instruction in electronic sources, the value of this type of learning strategy will become more evident.

Internet training:

Librarians are beginning to develop programs instructing on Internet, gopher, listservs, etc. While on some campuses the computer center takes over this training, the trend seems to be for librarians to teach the classes and leave technical aspects such as hardware questions and connection problems to the computer center. California Polytechnic State University has had a ten-week Internet class in place since 1991 (Rockman, 1993). The value of this type of training is that it stimulates students' interest in the wide variety of electronic resources that exist today. The more they are encouraged to explore what is out there, the less frightening the electronic environment will seem.

REFERENCE SERVICES

This area covers those types of services in which we provide one-on-one reference help. They may range from point-of-use instruction to more in-depth consultation appointments with a subject specialist. Every positive contact we make provides us with an opportunity to encourage users to feel free to search us out whenever they feel frustrated and overwhelmed.

Reference roving:
When librarians approach students at the terminals to offer help, the response is overwhelmingly positive. Usually this encourages a barrage of questions from those using the surrounding terminals. Librarians who provide this service find it effective in reaching out to those users who hesitate to approach the reference desk. When Boston College instituted this service and surveyed results, it found that 98 percent of users thought the assistance was useful and that it resulted in reduced demands on the staff (Bregman and Mento, 1992).

Peer tutoring:
The University of Michigan has been using its PIC (Peer Information Counseling) program for years now. Students staff the reference desk along with a reference librarian, answer the basic types of searching and directional questions, and refer to the librarian when necessary. These students also provide limited one-on-one instruction (MacAdam and Nichols, 1989).

Consultations:
Since we have merged government publications, social sciences, and humanities into one reference desk at UCSB, we cannot provide expertise in all subject areas. For questions that require more expertise, we hand out business cards at the reference desk and encourage users to make an appointment with the collection manager in their subject area for more in-depth research help.

Reference expert systems:
In addition to answering frequently asked general reference questions, these systems seem to help humanize the electronic environment for users. During these times of limited resources at the reference desk, we can ''speak'' to students through on-line reference help.

Libraries involved in downsizing must look at minimizing library anxiety as a way to improve public services during a time of change. Since the change is driven by dollars rather than chosen as a service goal, it is critical that this focus on the user serve as a bedrock. We can not rely on that single vital assumption—i.e., users feel sufficiently comfortable and welcome in the library to approach the staff and take advantage of their services. For many, the academic library experience is daunting and overwhelming. Librarians must consider how to best ensure that the clients we are committed to serving are not left wandering aimlessly in the information jungle.

BIBLIOGRAPHY

Bodi, Sonia. ''Teaching Effectiveness and Bibliographic Instruction: The Relevance of Learning Styles.'' *College and Research Libraries* 51 (March 1990): pp. 113-19.

Bregman, Adeane, and Barbara Mento. ''Reference Roving at Boston College.'' *College and Research Libraries News* 53:10 (November 1992): pp. 634-37.

Bristow, Ann. ''Academic Reference Service over Electronic Mail.'' *College and Research Libraries News* 53:10 (November 1992): pp. 631-37.

Brown, Mary. ''Library Attractibility Based on Social Styles of Users.''

Proceedings of the 54th Annual Meeting of the ASIS. Medford,
N.J.: Learned Information, 1991.

Bungard, Teresa, ed. "Reducing Library Anxiety and Defining Teaching." *Research Strategies* 5 (Summer 1987): pp. 146-48.

Canelas, Cathryn, and Lynn Westbrook. "BI in the Local High
School." *College & Research Libraries News* (March 1990): pp.
217-20.

Carande, Robert. "Expert Systems: Bibliographic Essay." *Choice* 30
(May 1993): pp. 1425-30.

Carlson, David, and Ruth H. Miller. "Librarians and Teaching
Faculty: Partners in Bibliographic Instruction." *College and Research
Libraries News* (November 1984): pp. 483-91.

Clement, Elaine, and Patricia A. Scott. "No Food, No Drink, No
Noise." *College and Research Libraries News* 55:2 (February 1994):
pp. 81-83.

Corno, Lynn, and Ruth Kanfer. "The Role of Volition in Learning
and Performance." In *Review of Research in Education,* vol. 19, ed.
Linda Darling-Hammond, pp. 301-42. Washington, D.C.: American Education Research Association, 1993.

Davis, Jinnie Y., and Stella Bentley. "Factors Affecting Faculty Perception of Academic Librarians." College and Research Libraries
News 40 (November 1979): pp. 527-32.

Dervin, Brenda, and Patricia Dewdney. "Neutral Questioning: A New
Approach to the Reference Interview." *RQ* (Summer 1986): pp.
506-13.

Feinman, Valerie Jackson. "Computers and Library Instruction: Expert Systems." *Computers in Libraries* 13:3 (March 1993): pp. 53-55.

Green, Donald, Joel Snell, and Anthony Parimanath. "Learning
Styles in Assessment of Students." *Perceptual and Motor Skills* 70
(1990): pp. 363-69.

Hensley, Randall. "Learning Style Theory and Learning Transfer
Principles During Reference Interview Instruction." *Library Trends*
39:3 (Winter 1991): pp. 203-09.

Joseph, Miriam E. "The Cure for Library Anxiety: It May Not Be What
You Think." *Catholic Library World* 63:2 (October/December 1991):
pp. 111-14.

Josey, E. J. "Library and Information Services for Cultural Minorities." *Libri* 35:4 (1985): pp. 320-32.

Keefer, Jane. "The Hungry Rats Syndrome: Library Anxiety, Information Literacy, and the Academic Reference Process." *RQ* 32:3
(Spring 1993): pp. 333-39.

Kuhlthau, Carol Collier. "Inside the Search Process: Information

Seeking from the User's Perspective." *Journal of the American Society for Information Science* 42:5 (June 1991): pp. 361-71.

Kuhlthau, Carol Collier. *Seeking Meaning: A Process Approach to Library and Information Services.* Norwood, NJ: Ablex Publishing Corp., 1993.

Kupersmith, John. "'Library Anxiety' and Library Graphics." *Research Strategies* (Winter 1987): pp. 36-38.

Lipow, Anne G. "Outreach to Faculty: Why and How." In *Working With Faculty in the New Electronic Library: Papers and Session Materials Presented at the Nineteenth National LOEX Library Instruction Conference* held at Eastern Michigan University 10 to 11 May 1991. Ann Arbor: Published for Learning Resources and Technologies, Eastern Michigan University, by Pieran Press, 1992.

MacAdam, Barbara, and Darlene Nichols. "Peer Information Counseling: An Academic Library Program for Minority Students." *Journal of Academic Librarianship* 15:4 (1989): pp. 204-9.

Mellon, Constance. "Library Anxiety: A Grounded Theory and Its Development." *College and Research Libraries News* (March 1986): pp. 160-65.

Millsap, Larry, and Terry Ellen Ferl. "Search Patterns of Remote Users: An Analysis of OPAC Transaction Logs." *Information Technology and Libraries* (September 1993): pp. 321-43.

Mood, Terry Ann. "Foreign Students and the Academic Library." *RQ* (Winter 1982): pp. 175-80.

Nahl-Jakobovits, Diane, and Leon A. Jakobovits. "Learning Principles and the Library Environment." *Research Strategies* (Spring 1990): pp. 74-81.

National Center for Education Statistics. Digest of Education Statistics. Washington, D.C.: U.S. Department of Health, Education and Welfare, 1993.

Nolan, Christopher W. "Closing the Reference Interview: Implications for Policy and Practice." *RQ* 31:4 (Summer 1992): pp. 513-23.

Piele, Linda J. "Reference Services and Staff Training for Patron-Use Software." *Library Trends* 40:1 (Summer 1991): pp. 97-119.

Rockman, Ilene F. "Teaching About the Internet: The Formal Course Option." *Reference Librarian* 39 (1993): pp. 65-75.

Sarkodie-Mensah, Kwasi. "Making Term Paper Counseling More Meaningful." *College and Research Libraries News* (November 1989): pp. 912-15.

Shapiro, Beth J., and Philip M. Marcus. "Library Use, Library Instruction, and User Success." *Research Strategies* 5:2 (Spring 1987): pp. 60-69.

Steffen, Susan Swords. "Designing Bibliographic Instruction Programs for Adult Students: The Schaffner Library Experience." *Illinois Libraries* 70 (December 1988): 644-49.

Stoffle, Carla J. "A New Library for the New Undergraduate." *Library Journal* 115:16 (1 October 1990): 47-50.

Stoffle, Carla J., Alan E. Guskin, and Joseph A. Boisse. "Teaching, Research, and Service: The Academic Library's Role." *New Directions for Teaching and Learning* 18 (June 1984): 3-14.

Tenopir, Carol. "Online Information Anxiety." *Library Journal* 115:13 (August 1990): 62-65.

Tomaiuolo, Nicholas G. "Redesigning Bibliographic Instruction for Adult Reentry Students: Emphasizing the Practical." *Reference Services Review* 18 (Spring 1990): 49-54.

Warmkessel, Marjorie Markoff, and Frances M. Carothers. "Collaborative Learning and Bibliographic Instruction." *Journal of Academic Librarianship* 19:1 (1993): 4-7.

6

Peer Information Counselors: Experienced Students Assist Librarians in Extending Bibliographic Instruction Programs

Karen Downing
University of Michigan

At the University of Michigan, we are trying to stretch our BIbang for the buck—and, at the same time, diversify the manner in which we deliver bibliographic instruction. At the Undergraduate Library, for the last three years, we have been utilizing the talents and energy of our Peer Information Counselors as well as our graduate student interns and reference assistants to assist librarians with bibliographic instruction delivery. We do this in many forms and to different degrees, but all efforts combined have allowed us to reach many more students than we could ever reach without their help. I'd like to start off by telling you just a bit about our campus and our library to give some context to our situation.

The University of Michigan's undergraduate population is approximately 22,000. We have gone from reaching 3,618 students through our BI efforts in 1990 to reaching 8,914 students in 1993. Because we feel BI is so important, and because our librarians are continually asked to do more with less (the library has undergone personnel cuts for the last several years), we understand the necessity of being creative with the delivery of BI to our target population.

We used to define bibliographic instruction very narrowly in terms of course-related, classroom instruction. Today, University of Michigan Undergraduate librarians define BI as a broad series of instructional activities. We include all activities where reference and instruction staff are teaching recruited or currently enrolled undergraduate students information literacy skills. This includes:

- Traditional classroom instruction,
- Summer and fall orientation sessions for new students,
- Semester long classes taught by librarians,
- Small group instructional sessions with our athletic department,
- Summer recruitment programs for junior and high school students,
- Teaching Assistant classes for those who will teach undergrads,
- Student sponsored events such as FestiFall (a big outdoor, information fair on the campus square,) and
- Special presentations to students groups such as BSU (Black Student Union), SALSA (Socially Active Latino Student Association) etc.

This list is not complete, but it gives you an idea of the range of instructional activities in which we are involved. The undergraduate library partners with many academic units, including the Athletic Department, the Office of Admissions, the Office of Orientation, the Center for Research on Teaching and Learning (a faculty resource center), the Minority Engineering Program Office, the Instructional Technology Center, the Office of Multicultural and Academic Affairs, The Comprehensive

Studies Program (a multidisciplinary academic unit devoted to retention of students of color), Minority Student Services, the English Composition Board, and others. Within these partnerships, we have developed instructional components to reach undergraduate students.

Of the 22,000 undergraduate students, approximately 20 percent are students of color. Back in the mid-80's the university began to address issues of recruitment and retention of undergraduate students of color by funding special programs throughout the university. During this time, the Undergraduate Library submitted a proposal to fund the Peer Information Counseling Program. The proposal was funded out of the Presidential Initiatives fund beginning in 1985. By 1988 the program was judged a success by the campus and the money became part of the libraries base budget. The original intent of the program was threefold:

1. To provide an opportunity for several undergraduate students of color to become extremely information literate through intensive training and work at the reference desk and in the Academic Resource Center (a computer training and study center within the Undergraduate Library).
2. To have those students serve as library role models to other undergraduate students.
3. To make the undergraduate library a more welcoming and less intimidating place for undergraduate students of color.

Since that time, the number of PIC students has risen 12 to 13 each year. We have been fortunate enough to have PIC students stay with us two, three, and even four years, and we have expanded the role of some PIC students to include various instructional responsibilities. Of those 12 to 13 PIC students, second, third, and fourth year students who express interest in teaching are encouraged to participate in our instructional programs.

At the same time, our reference and instruction department had just begun to explore the possibility of utilizing graduate students in the School of Information and Library Studies (reference interns and reference assistants) to supplement our teaching staff and give SILS students hands-on opportunities to teach. In this past academic year we have really hit our stride with that effort, developing a new bibliographic instruction internship with SILS. SILS students receive credit for participating in the internship program. During the course of one semester a particular department or class is targeted by the SILS intern. A framework for gathering information about the department, meeting with the faculty and/or chair, and devising and delivering instructional options, are the outcomes. Out of this internship program we have strengthened our ties with the Psychology Department, Political Science Department, and Residential College (a small liberal arts college within the larger university setting).

One impetus for turning to supplemental staff or instructional assistance was purely serendipitous. In 1991 a former PIC student expressed an interest to me in assisting with a class for which I was preparing. It was an interdisciplinary class about gender and science that she had taken the year before. She was familiar with the course work, assignments, and knew what sorts of problems she had encountered while doing her library research. I heartily agreed to co-teach the class with her, thinking that her presence in the classroom might put the students at ease much the same way PIC students' presence eases fears at the reference desk. In a pre-class preparation meeting we discussed how to split up the teaching responsibilities, and she filled me in on her experiences. We also talked about active learning versus lecturing. The class went like a charm. As I was wrapping it up, I asked the students if they had any questions. As usual there were a few, but I suspected there were many more that went unasked. I then dismissed the class. Within seconds, a third of the class members were swarming around the PIC student with urgent questions! In addition to making me feel older than the hills, it sent a clear message as to how intimidated students feel in asking questions of non-peers. This was a real revelation for me, being one of the younger instruction librarians. The experience led me to raise the subject to other UGli librarians about the prospect of including PIC students in the classroom. Thus we began to explore ways in which we could use the talents of PIC students to supplement our instructional program. Valarie and I would like to share a few of these examples now.

COMPUTERIZED CLASSROOM INSTRUCTION

Since 1991 a lot of things have changed in our staff patterns and our physical environment. We now have a fully computerized classroom where we do 90 percent of our teaching. We have 25 computer terminals in the room. Trying to teach in front of 25-40 students who are at differing levels of computer literacy is difficult at best. Some of the students are inevitably lost, some are ahead, equipment fails; it can become an instructional nightmare! Having an extra body in the classroom is very important to keep the students on track. It allows us to move the class along in a timely way, and it provides support to those who might otherwise get left behind. Since sparing two librarians for each class is an unrealistic option, we have asked PIC students and reference assistants/interns to assist us in this way. They are also on hand to teach the students about the services of the PIC program and reference. While we have no written evaluation of the difference in satisfaction levels of classes with and without PIC students and interns, observational evidence shows us time and time again that undergraduate students open up to the staff. Educational research also strongly supports our experiences (Kemp, Martino, Saunders).

ATHLETIC DEPARTMENT INSTRUCTION

Another significant use of PIC students in our instructional program is work they do for the Athletic Department. For the last two years we have been doing different types of instruction for all first year student athletes. This includes over 120 student athletes each year. In a series of 3-6 classroom sessions, we introduce them to information gathering strategies, library services, and our online catalog and indexes.

More intense three-on-one instruction is done solely by PIC

students, for the freshman football players whose schedules in the Fall semester are extremely hectic. Valarie's brother Virgil Burton has been our instructional guru here since we began this effort. Due to Virgil's personal ties with many of the student athletes, and his exceptional information literacy skills, I have felt very comfortable making Virgil the library's contact with the football team's academic advisor. Virgil meets with the athletic department contact to review lesson plans and learning styles/levels of the various student athletes. Together, with input from me and other librarians, an instructional plan is developed and adapted according to each groups' needs. This won PIC and the library important support from a very powerful department on campus. The athletic department is so appreciative of our efforts they agreed last year to fund one PIC student position to support their students' library needs.

SUMMER BRIDGE PROGRAM

Every July and August the University runs a summer bridging program for just-graduated high school seniors who will be freshmen in the Fall semester. The Bridge Program, run by our Comprehensive Studies Program (CSP) office helps facilitate these 60-70 students' transition from high school to college. Bridge students spend a half summer semester living on campus and taking a variety of for-credit classes. Because these students develop excellent peer group cohesion, relationships with faculty and knowledge of the campus community, the library often draws form Bridge "graduates" for its Peer Information Counseling staff. In turn, the Bridge program often borrows back PIC students during the summer to fill their peer advisor positions. Peer advisors live in the residence halls with Bridge students, guide them through the transition, and give them the benefit of their experiences. Because of this exceptionally symbiotic relationship, for the last three years we have asked PIC students to assist with the series of classes the undergraduate library conducts for the Bridge students. PIC students are perfect role models for these students. They assist with the classroom instruction and are also available in the library for follow-up sessions where the Bridge students work on library exercises that count as their mid-term examination. PIC students are available in the residence hall where they can show Bridge students how to dial MIRLYN. This PIC instructional support has improved our Bridge instruction markedly. Since PIC students have been assisting, the quality and comprehension of the exercises has increased tremendously. The feedback we have received from the students and faculty of CSP has been extremely positive.

MEPO
(MINORITY ENGINEERING PROGRAM OFFICE)

The Minority Engineering Program Office sponsors a Summer Engineering Academy each summer for under-represented students of color. The academy offers a highly-structured curriculum which exposes students to the many disciplines and career opportunities of engineering. One component, the Professionals in Training Program, is provided for incoming first year students of the University of Michigan's School of Engineering. Each year, the Undergraduate Library staff meet with the MEPO staff to develop instructional sessions for their specific needs.

K/C/P (KING/CHAVEZ/PARKS)

The King/Chavez/Parks College Day Spring Visitation Program is designed to give African American, Latino American, and Native American high school students from neighboring districts a sense of what university life is like. These students come to the University of Michigan for a day long visit where they tour the university to learn more about college in order to encourage these students to consider a college education. Along with the School of Information and Library Studies, our goal was to provide the students with information on how to expand their college and career options, impress upon them the importance of information literacy, and give them a little background into who we are and what we do. Lester, another PIC student, and I prepared packets of information which included bibliographies of books by and about people of color and short biographies on people of color. These bibliographies and biographies were compiled and updated by former and current PIC students. We also talked about what it was like to be an undergraduate working in a library. The best part was sharing with them my experiences in a library prior to college. They seemed very interested in the fact that I first began working a school library way back in the third grade and also worked at a Detroit public branch library my junior and senior years of high school.

Because there are many more interesting situations in which PIC students are delivering bibliographic instruction, and because our time is short, we have prepared a short description of some of these programs.

It is realistic to suggest that some librarians may see undergraduate or even graduate students teaching, or even working on the reference desk as a threat to the very core of what we as librarians hold as unique to our profession. However, to those who are wary I would assure that PIC students in no way supplant or replace librarians in these functions, they merely expand and improve our current services. By inviting experienced students to assist with the delivery of instruction, we can reach a much more diverse group of undergraduates and recruits. At the same time, we have provided these students with exceptional role models, and allowed for growth and satisfaction within the PIC students' jobs.

A word of caution. A program that works in our institution may not work at another. Because of SILS, and because of our University's explicit commitment to the idea of a multicultural campus, we feel lucky and confident that our program is right for us. We do, however, have much work to do yet.

I believe we are at a critical point now in the development of PIC instructional activities. Traditionally, PIC students have worked primarily at the reference desk and in our Academic Resource Center teaching in one-on-one situations; functioning in a capacity which they are formally trained. The day has come where relying on their assistance in order to deliver BI services is no longer a series of experiments. Meaning, as a department, our instruction librarians must take the time this summer to develop a more formalized PIC training and evaluation program for group instruction. In preliminary discussions, a decision was reached to adapt the training syllabus currently in use by interns, assistants, and librarians. Whatever form it takes, we will want to ensure that PIC students feel completely comfortable when asked to teach, and that they are better prepared to face the future challenges of bibliographic instruction.

7

Burrowing into BI: The Care and Feeding of a Library Gopher

Andrea L. Duda
University of California at Santa Barbara

The Internet gopher was developed by programmers at the University of Minnesota in 1991. Today there are over 4,000 gopher servers around the world being run by computing centers, professional organizations, academic departments, commercial organizations, and libraries.

A gopher provides an easy-to-use front end to Internet resources. A gopher user has access to documents, programs, sounds, images, databases, and other Internet resources. Users don't have to remember the computer address of their favorite database or image collection; the gopher keeps track of that information for them. All the user has to do is select an item from a menu.

From time to time various people (mostly librarians) have proposed that Internet resources should be cataloged in order to provide better access to them. While trying to catalog the ever-changing resources on the Internet seems an impossible task, gophers provide a very simple and very personalized framework for organizing the Internet. Users can take advantage of the gopher's ability to organize and locate resources by using subject-oriented gophers (like the Davidson Library's InfoSurf or the North Carolina State University Library Without Walls) or by using Veronica, a tool that searches gopher menus around the world.

Gopher servers run on a variety of platforms, including UNIX, Macintosh, PC, VMS, and Windows. The software is available by anonymous ftp1 and there is no charge for getting or using the gopher software.

The gopher software comes with minimal documentation. While it's not difficult for a programmer or a UNIX guru to set up a gopher server, the rest of us benefit greatly by working with someone who has already set up a gopher and can answer questions and provide advice. The next best way to get information is to use electronic communication. There are gopher newsgroup and gopher mailing lists including gophernews and go4lib-l, a list devoted to library gophers.[2]

When the software is set up, adding items to the gopher is a straightforward process. You don't have to be a programmer to design or maintain a gopher; you just have to be able to find basic information, such as the type of resource (a file or a telnet session, for example), its host, and its path. A good gopher starts with a good initial design. It is important to decide on the purpose of the gopher and its audience. Then, long before you add a single item to a gopher menu, spend time working out its overall structure.

When you are working on the gopher's design, take time to explore gopherspace. Get to a link for "all the Gophers in the World," and then follow the links wherever they may take you. In your travels you will see some gophers that are very appealing, drawing you in to spend time exploring them. With others, however, one quick look is all it takes before you want to move on to something more interesting.

Some of the factors that contribute to an inviting opening menu include:

1. It's short, not more than one screen.
2. Menu entries are clear; you don't find entries with titles like "Miscellaneous" or "Interesting Stuff" that give you no clue as to their content.
3. Menu entries appear in a logical order, not necessarily alphabetically. Too many gopher developers have not figured out how to specify the order of gopher items.
4. The menu uses upper and lower case to make them easy to read. The fact that a good opening menu follows the same principles does not mean that they all look alike. Consider the North Carolina State University Library Without Walls and the InfoSlug system from the University of California, Santa Cruz. The two gophers are organized quite differently, yet both are efficient and easy to use.

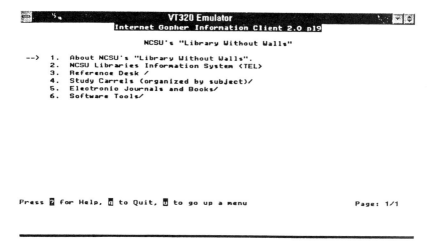

Fig. 7-1. Opening Menu of North Carolina State University's Library Without Walls.

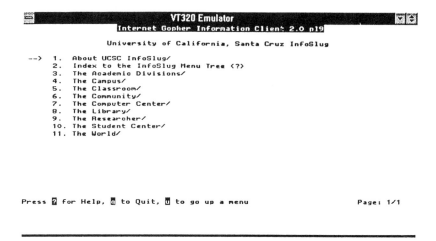

Fig. 7-2. Opening Menu of the University of California, Santa Cruz InfoSlug.

The top of the menu should include an item with a title like "About This Gopher." This item should include information about the purpose of the gopher and its intended audience. This item should also include information about the gopher's organization and the name and e-mail address of someone to contact if a user has questions or discovers problems.

After developing the opening screen, it is important to carry a good design through the rest of the gopher. Try to have the entries follow a logical order. Remember that the people using the gopher will have to follow your logic in reaching the information they want. It may be helpful to include an organization scheme in the "About" file so that users will have a sense of the developer's overall vision.

One thing to keep in mind when adding items to the gopher is Veronica. Veronica is a tool that works with gophers to search the titles on gopher menus around the world.

Veronica is a huge step forward in making the information in gophers accessible to users. Its drawback is that it is totally dependent on the titles that gopher developers have given to the items in their gophers. A user searching on "Astronomy," for example, would miss a menu item with a name like "Black Holes and Other Space Phenomena." Thus, gopher developers should avoid names that substitute wit for information.

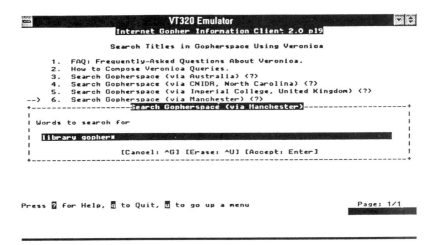

Fig. 7-3. A sample Veronica search.

It's important to remember that Veronica searches the menu titles only, not the text of the documents that are included. A user searching Veronica gets back a list of the menu items that match the search. She doesn't see the other items that appear on the same menu, nor does she see the hierarchy that led to that particular menu item. Thus it's important to try and include enough information in the item's name to provide the context that Veronica searchers need. This step is easy to forget and not always possible to carry out, but the extent to which gopher developers follow through on this makes Veronica a more useful search tool.

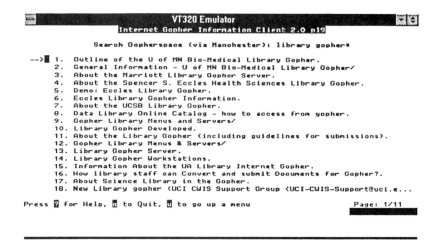

Fig. 7-4. The results of a Veronica search. The user selects items from the menu that appears.

If you make the decision to create a gopher, make a commitment to its continued development. There is a time commitment involved in maintaining a gopher. Resources disappear and should be removed. Others move and the links need to be changed. And, of course, new resources are constantly appearing.

It's important to keep up with new resources and there are several ways to do this. One excellent source is the HYTEL-L3 mailing list. It's designed to help people keep Hytelnet (an Internet navigation tool) up-to-date. New resources accessible using the "telnet" command are regularly announced. The alt.internet.services newsgroup often includes announcements of new Internet resources mixed in among the quantities of messages with little relevant content. New resources are often announced on PACS-L4, GOVDOC-L5, and a variety of other mailing lists. It helps if the library has a network of people watching for new resources and bringing them to the attention of the gopher developer.

When the framework for the gopher is in place, you may start to find new uses for it. When InfoSurf, the Davidson

Library gopher opened to the public in March 1993, it provided access to resources both inside and outside the library. Internal resources included pamphlets, reference guides, and newsletters.

It wasn't long before we discovered that InfoSurf was a good place to make the minutes of meetings available to the library staff. Then we realized that it could help us to solve a couple of different problems.

The first problem relates to our library skills classes. The Davidson Library offers a one-credit library skills class. It covers the basics of using library tools like our online catalogs, printed indexes, CD-ROMs, and several different article databases. Every quarter we offer seven sections of this class. Every quarter the classes fill quickly, and every quarter the instructors know that the first day of classes will bring a group of students asking if there is room for them to add the class.

This problem could be resolved by simply adding more sections of the class. Unfortunately, many librarians were lost to the three early retirement programs offered by the University of California. We simply do not have enough people to teach additional sections.

The second problem relates to remote users of the library. People who come into the library can pick up guides to using the PEGASUS and MELVYL online systems; they can talk with a librarian to resolve problems. But how do you provide this kind of assistance to people who don't come into the building? They are limited to receiving the information available through the help screens on the online systems.

The sevices of gopher were enlisted to resolve both of these problems. By putting library skills information onto the gopher, those students unable to attend class can still receive instruction. People accessing the library from their homes, offices, or computer labs can retrieve the classroom instruction. With gopher the information is available when the patron needs it, even if it is at times when the library is closed. Developing the library skills tutorial required a time commitment up front. In the future, efforts will be needed to maintain and update the program. But the investment of time will be minimal and the capacity to provide instruction to patrons will be limitless.

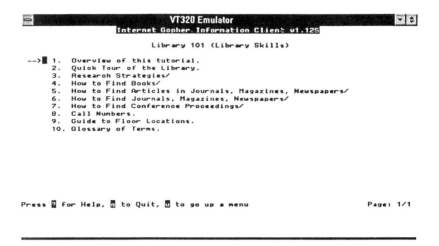

Fig. 7-5. The opening menu of the library skills tutorial.

The tutorial developed follows the format of a library skills class. After a section describing the tutorial, coverage moves on to describe library service desks, research strategies, how to find various kinds of materials, call numbers, floor locations, and a glossary of terms.

In the sections describing how to use the PEGASUS and MELVYL systems to find books, journals, and conference proceedings, links are included to the OPACS so that users could try out their new skills. In each section we also included an item where users can test what they've learned.

Developing a library skills tutorial on InfoSurf has clearly shown the pluses and minuses of using a gopher. A gopher enables you to create as many links to information as you like. Depending on the complexity of the material to be presented, there can be many files or just a few. You can present the information in any order. This enables you to present information on searching the online catalog, for example, followed by a menu item that connects the user to the OPAC using a telnet session. If a particular piece of information fits in more than one section, it is possible to create the file just once but have many links to it. For example, information on how to obtain materials through interlibrary loan might fit under the sections on locating books, locating articles, and locating conference proceedings.

Another advantage to using gopher for bibliographic instruction is that users can pick and choose the information they need at the time they need it. A user who wants to know how to use the MELVYL article databases can get that information while skipping other parts of the tutorial. If a user wishes to go through the whole tutorial sequentially, that option is also available. A user can spend as much time as needed to read and understand the information. Finally, barring computer problems, the gopher is available to users 24 hours a day, seven days a week.

There are two major disadvantages to using a gopher for BI. First, the gopher does not provide an interactive tutorial. Users select files and read them, then move on to the next file. While we can present a test, for example, the user can only read it or print it out. She cannot interact with the computer to take the test or review sections that were missed.

A bigger disadvantage in using the gopher is that all of the information must be presented as straight ASCII text. A gopher does not allow the use of different sized fonts, highlighting, underlining, or italicizing. This means that one must be creative in finding ways to present the information in a clear and visually pleasing way. White space is very important, and characters like * = or # can be used to separate items or draw attention to information.

Using a gopher to provide a library skills tutorial has allowed us to overcome problems with reduced staffing and reaching remote users.

Gophers are a wonderful way of providing a whole world of information to library patrons. A well-designed gopher brings to electronic information the library's traditional goals of acquiring information, organizing it, and making it accessible to patrons.

Like any other library resource, developing a gopher requires a commitment of time and effort. The time is well worth it, however, when you so easily expand the library's resources.

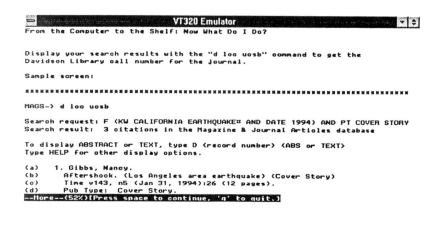

Fig. 7-6. The gopher offers limited ways of explaining the information to users. Here we used letters to identify the pieces of information the user needs.

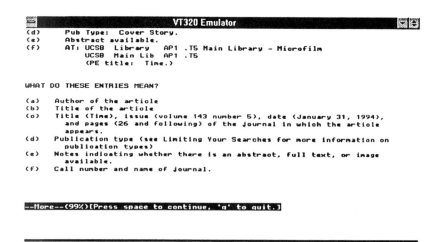

Fig. 7-7. The gopher limits displays to ASCII text.

Librarians bring a perspective to the world of electronic information that's different from the perspectives of programmers or computer support people. We are able to bring the same principles that apply to organizing print information to gophers, making them easy to use and understand. Library gophers are an excellent resource for library patrons as well as a contribution to the promised information highway.

ENDNOTES

1. ftp boombox.micro.umn,edu in the pub/gopher directory
2. See comp.infosystems.gopher,gopher-news@boombox.micro.umn,edu, and go4lib-l@ucsbvm.bitnet
3. HYTEL-L@kentvm.bitnet
4. PACS-L@uhupvm1.bitnet
5. GOVDOC-L@psuvm.bitnet

8

Toward Innovative Instructional Options for the 1990's: A Process of Strategic Collaboration in the Science/Technology Libraries of Harvard University

Donald G. Frank
Cabot Science Library, Harvard University

INTRODUCTION

There is a critical need for organizational collaboration among the science libraries at Harvard University. The need underscores the fundamental rationale for the compilation of strategic recommendations to facilitate communication and to improve reference and instructional services. With an intense decentralized tradition, cooperative efforts among these libraries have been historically minimal. By 1992, economic, political, and social realities accented the need to consider alternative organizational collaborations and structures in order to improve informational and instructional services and to progress toward user-focused initiatives. These realities and the elements of the resulting collaborative process constitute the central themes of this paper.

THE UNIVERSITY'S DECENTRALIZED ORGANIZATIONAL STRUCTURE

The concept of decentralization underscores the essential characteristics or features of Harvard University's organizational structure. From an overall organizational perspective, Harvard has been decentralized for more than 350 years. Harvard's various colleges and schools have, more or less, operated independently. The concepts of autonomy and independence constitute a fundamental organizational value. Political and financial independence are especially valued by Harvard's colleges and schools. While these concepts are also valued at other colleges and universities, the appreciation is probably accented at Harvard. The results of this decentralized organizational structure have been extraordinary over time.

Nearly all colleges and universities have been coping or dealing with a variety of economic constraints and realities. Harvard's economic base and resources have been and remain extensive. Nonetheless, fiscal contingencies are beginning to surface among the decentralized colleges and schools. In a recent letter to the general faculties, Neil L. Rudenstine, Harvard's President, noted the University's "constrained resources." According to President Rudenstine, "we live at a time when knowledge and information are growing so fast, and when resources are so constrained, that no single institution—not even one of Harvard's size and breadth—can hope to cover every field of learning, or try to meet every perceived need."[1] He discusses "standards of excellence" and states that excellence "requires constant adaptation to changing realities. . . . [2]

Excellence is critically important at Harvard and ranks as one of the fundamental organizational values. President Rudenstine asserts that concepts such as coordination, facilitation, and integration will be requisites to continue or maintain the current or desired standards of excellence. These concepts underlie the recurring themes in Dr. Rudenstine's report to Harvard's Board of Overseers, a report summarizing the results of a two-year University-wide planning process. The need to integrate and realign University resources is continually emphasized, "especially in those areas where it is essential for us to plan and act more as a single institution rather than a confederation of separate parts."[3] Moreover, the University needs to "focus . . . more on developing our capacities to coordinate, to consolidate, and to improve the programs we already offer and the resources we already possess."[4]

The concepts of coordination, integration, and excellence are imbedded in President Rudenstine's list of institutional goals for Harvard University. In this summary of institutional goals, Harvard's fundamental purposes focus on and encompass the essential elements of "excellence, openness, [and] service."

- To bring the University's different parts closer together, so that we can live and act more effectively as a single institution. Sustaining the strength of every individual school and unit remains essential: but our ability to achieve this goal will depend, more and more, on our ability to reinforce the strength of Harvard as a whole.
- To redesign many of our first-degree and advanced educational programs, especially but not only in professional education. A central purpose here is to strengthen the links among research, teaching, learning, and practice. As our world and the major professions continue to change in fundamental ways, so too must education change.
- To invest substantially in the teaching mission of undergraduate education in the arts and sciences, and indeed in the programs of all our schools. Nearly every faculty or school plans to place substantial emphasis on the development of teaching methods that stimulate active inquiry and expand the opportunities for advanced independent work on the part of students: more small-scale discussion groups or seminars; a greater use of challenging case studies; more effective uses of information technology; and more possibilities for internships and field work.
- To increase our understanding of—and our ability to help

address—pressing problems that now confront our own society as well as many others. These include (among others) the difficulties faced by public school systems, problems related to health care, threats to the environment, the state of the world's economy and its political institutions, and the need to further international understanding in the cause of peace.

- To sustain Harvard as a strong human as well as academic institution: residential, open, diverse, and committed to creating a community in which individuals and groups learn from one another outside the classroom as well as inside. Maintaining our strong financial aid programs is one critical part of this effort. Sustaining close and fruitful relations with our neighboring communities—Cambridge, Boston, and beyond—represents another important part.
- To continue our drive to achieve better management of the resources we already possess. This includes the need to seek economies, to make selective reductions, and to consolidate programs or activities when appropriate.[5]

Phrases such as "more effectively as a single institution" and "the need to seek economies, to make selective reductions, and to consolidate programs or activities" have probably generated some concern. Will excellence be compromised?

ORGANIZATIONAL STRUCTURE OF THE SCIENCE/TECHNOLOGY LIBRARIES

Harvard's decentralized academic libraries are representative of the University's organizational structure. With nearly 100 libraries, the decentralized organizational structure is obvious. Currently, these specific libraries are categorized as science libraries: Biological Laboratories Library; Botany Libraries; Cabot Science Library; Center for Astrophysics Libraries; Chemistry Library; Countway Library of Medicine; Kummel Geological Sciences Library; McKay Applied Sciences Library; Mathematics Library; Museum of Comparative Zoology Library; Physics Research Library; Psychology Research Library; Statistics Library;

and the Tozzer Library. The Psychology Research Library and the Tozzer Library provide extensive support for the social sciences as well. In addition to these libraries, there are approximately 20 other libraries or "information centers" that support the sciences.

In a paper on "gateway libraries," Harvard's Associate Librarian for Public Services, Lawrence Dowler, notes that the "Harvard libraries, indeed the University, have often been compared to a federation of autonomous states."[6] Use of "autonomous" is appropriate in a discussion of gateway concepts at Harvard. As the various colleges and schools are protective of their autonomy and independence, the numerous decentralized libraries are similarly protective of their budgets, collections, and associated informational programs and services. This is accented in the various science libraries as most are not organizational elements of Harvard's College Library. They exist as autonomous units and usually focus their efforts on a specific clientele (one academic department, for example). Historically, cooperation has not been valued.

Unfortunately, in academia, this lack of cooperation or collaboration is not unusual. Too frequently, competition tends to prevail over cooperation. Some competition is needed. In the University, Henry Rosovsky, Dean of Harvard's Faculty of Arts & Sciences for more than a decade, notes the positive and negative consequences of institutional competitiveness. Colleges and universities usually compete for faculty, students, and available funds. Quality in the institution's instructional and research programs and the associated (and desired) academic prestige depends on good faculty and students as well as substantial and needed funds. A sense of competition among and within colleges and universities tends to promote institutional quality. Overall, institutional competition has "prevented complacency and spurred the drive for excellence and change."[7]

Several of the negative consequences of institutional competitiveness are also noted by Dr. Rosovsky. Specifically, these include "too much movement by professorial stars from one university to another in relentless pursuit of personal gain; a consequently lower level of institutional loyalty; invidious comparisons between fields giving excessive advantages to those subjects where market power is strong (as in computer sciences vs. English); and . . . the deleterious effects of a Wall Street mentality that focuses too much on short-term highly visible achievements at the expense of the long run and the unfashionable.''[8] Competitive realities and the associated implications exist at all administrative levels of colleges and universities and do not necessarily contribute to a sense of cooperation or collaboration. These realities and implications are integral elements in the historical evolution of Harvard's libraries and, particularly, of Harvard's science libraries.

Given all the science libraries and various "information centers," it has been, historically, difficult to collaborate. A good number of these libraries have been associated with specific academic departments and have been operational for decades. With libraries being funded by the academic departments, cooperative initiatives have not been perceived as important or necessary. Occasionally, incentives to cooperate have been subjugated by a sense of economic independence. In the past, organizational values related to competition or independence have dominated the collaborative values.

What is the College Library? Most science libraries are not organizational elements of the College Library. The College Library is one of the major organizational units of the University Library and includes the Widener Library (focus on the humanities and social sciences), Cabot Science Library, Fine Arts Library, Harvard-Yenching Library, Hilles Library, Houghton Library, Kummel Geological Sciences Library, Lamont Library, Littauer Library, Music Library, and Tozzer Library (anthropology). Only three of the libraries in the sciences are organizational elements of Harvard's College Library, specifically the Cabot Science Library, Kummel Geological Sciences Library, and Tozzer Library. The other science libraries are departmental libraries in the Faculty of Arts & Sciences or are affiliated with the various colleges and schools. All of Harvard's libraries are "loosely" organized under the University Library, a comprehensive administrative unit. Overall, it's a complex organizational structure.

So, the organizational structure of Harvard's science and technology libraries is complex and fractious. Centralization and uniformity do not necessarily underscore the policies, collections, and services of these libraries. Historically (and too frequently), cooperation and collaboration among the libraries have not been valued as organizational priorities. The implications of these policies and practices have been dramatic and numerous.

IMPLICATIONS OF THE DECENTRALIZED ORGANIZATIONAL STRUCTURE

A positive and significant implication of Harvard's decentralized structure focuses on proximity to users. As the libraries are organizational elements of academic departments or divisions and are usually located within the department/division, the staffs and information sources are readily available. Faculty and students are able to confer with librarians and to access available information sources with relative ease. Informal user needs assessment is conducted on a day-to-day basis. Librarians and users develop and refine ongoing and occasionally sophisticated "information-based relationships." Users tend to see the library as their library. They are advocates of the library and usually supportive of the library's needs.

President Rudenstine's comments underscore the need to examine "Harvard as a whole." His statements focus on the importance of excellence in education, the relevance of the various colleges and schools, and the realities of budgets that are not fiscally unlimited. Lack of cooperation and collaboration can only serve to create negative implication for the decentralized organizational structure of science libraries. With different administrative structures and with budgets usually tied to specific academic departments or divisions, the impetus to consider or generate collaborative programmatic activities, with some exceptions, has not been particularly evident. For decades, the funds needed for collections and services (especially collections) in the libraries have been sufficient. As a result, the rationale to cooperate with another library (or with other libraries) has not been commonly discussed as one of the relevant priorities. Nonetheless, current fiscal realities as well as the dramatic changes in informational services and technologies have accented the need to consider cooperative activities programs.

COLLECTIONS-BASED MODEL
AND THE FORCES OF CHANGE

Organizational values underlie the fundamental activities and programs of all libraries or systems of libraries. In general, Harvard's libraries have focused on collections for more than 350 years. Essentially, it's been a collections-based system of libraries. Activities associated with the cultivation and development of collections define or characterize a basic and important organizational value. The collections, including those in the sciences, are excellent.

Since the mid- to late-1980s, changes in the processes of scholarly communication, the critical need for access to information in the sciences, and serials inflation have dramatically affected the collections-based model in the science libraries. The impact varies from library to library, but is a significant reality for all of the libraries. The roles and responsibilities of professionals in libraries are changing as the procedures used by scholars to communicate, including the various forms of publication, change to reflect scholarly and institutional needs. These changes and modifications are being studied, and noted in the current literature. Mary Reichel's dissertation (1992) on "Scholarly Communication and Information Needs in 2001" is a notable effort to delineate the degrees of impact in the humanities, fine arts, sciences, and social sciences. This study concludes that the processes of scholarly communication in the sciences and some areas of the social sciences will continue to change dramatically. In particular, scholars in the sciences indicate that these changes will probably accelerate significantly.[9] As the processes of communication used by scholars and educators in the sciences continue to change, the composition, structure, and format of the information needed for instructional and research needs will also change. A collections-based model will be affected.

Access to information in the sciences is usually as critical as the actual information. Information is frequently scanned and processed by scientists via electronic access. Currently, effective electronic access to the major databases in the sciences is not provided for Harvard's faculty and students. A significant number of users are frustrated. Some are simply not aware that effective access to relevant information is not currently provided. As the pressures to provide realistic access to databases increase, some funds usually allocated to the traditional collections will be reallocated to cover access-related expenditures. The collections-based model will be affected by the pressures to provide effective access.

Collections in academic libraries across the nation have been affected by intense serials inflation for nearly a decade. Serials in the scientific and technical academic disciplines and some areas of the social sciences have been particularly affected by these inflationary pressures. Activities associated with serials cancellations as well as the possible scenarios for shared resources have become important issues in academic libraries. At the local, regional, and national levels, scholarly communication processes have been affected by serials inflation and related cancellation efforts. Selected serials have been canceled in several of Harvard's science libraries. Overall, cancellations have not been significant to date. Nonetheless, acquisitions or information related budgets are not necessarily keeping up with continued inflationary pressures. The collections-based model will be affected by these incessant economic pressures.

ASSOCIATED RELEVANT FACTORS

Leadership is obviously an essential component in any library or system of libraries. The ability to provide focus and direction, generates a shared vision for the future, and inspires others to define priorities and strategies in to collaborative efforts to attain their desired goals. Paul E. Peters, President of the Coalition for Networked Information, presented a paper at one of Harvard's open forums in which he discussed desirable or essential elements of leadership for librarians and other information specialists. Emphasis was placed on the importance of exploration and discovery over data analysis. Concepts of competition and acquisitions need to be replaced by the realities of cooperation and constructive partnerships. Finally, the organizational structure needs to be continuously examined and essentially "reinvented." In his concluding comments, Mr. Peters articulated that librarians as leaders must be able to deal with political ambiguities and must be willing to take risks in the development of a shared vision for the future.[10]

Among Harvard's science and technology libraries, lack of a shared vision for the future has been problematic. With the decentralized structure and with the various administrative structures, cooperative activities have traditionally been uncommon. Collaborative efforts have occurred, but usually in response to specific crises. Overall, cooperation and collaboration have not been fundamental organizational values. A shared vision for the future has not been developed or generated. Lack of this shared vision has been a significant problem for Harvard's science libraries. In reality, a lack of overall leadership has been a dramatic problem.

According to Webster's, insularity connotes the "quality or state of being an island or consisting of islands."[11] The concept is defined in terms of "isolation." Occasionally, one listens to comments on the concept of insularity in relation to libraries, including those in the sciences, at Harvard University. This is probably normal and expected. It's Harvard University! The collections are excellent and the professional expertise is exceptional. But, with a degree of traditional insularity. Considering the resources available within Harvard's academic community, the rationale or impetus to look outwardly for other ideas or methodologies has been less than obvious. This tradition is gradually changing (from inwardly to outwardly), but has been occasionally problematic and has affected services-related efforts and issues in the scientific and technical libraries.

As the various academic disciplines tend to coalesce or converge, a decentralized organizational structure of autonomous libraries will probably "struggle" in efforts to provide effective, state-of-the-art informational services. If students are regularly forced to go to 3-5 or 6-8 libraries to access and/or obtain needed information, barriers to desired information become quite significant. As time passes, these barriers become patterns and processes that are frequently problematic. In a sense, creation of the "universal information workstation" becomes more difficult. Interdisciplinary activities and tendencies will probably continue to accelerate, especially in the sciences (the environmental sciences, for example), necessitating elevated degrees of inter- and intra-organizational collaboration.

Independence is usually perceived as desirable. If libraries or other organizational entities are economically independent, the motivation or need to participate in collaborative efforts is probably less obvious. With different economic bases, the budgets and economic contingencies of Harvard's science libraries have varied from library to library. As a result, the impetus to cooperate actively and to examine the overall picture has varied from library to library.

The concept of trust is critical to effective teamwork and contributes significantly to a positive work environment. A lack of trust will affect communications among individuals as well as libraries. This occasionally surfaces among the science libraries (and between these libraries and the College Library).

The combination of the above forces of change as well as the associated factors or problems contributed to an atmosphere in which organizational values, relative priorities, and fiscal realities could be critically discussed and examined. Moreover, strategic planning for the College Library was imminent.

A SIGNIFICANT CATALYST FOR CHANGE

A major catalyst for change occurred in 1990. Richard De Gennaro assumed responsibility for the College Library. Within months after his arrival, a considerable number of librarians and support staff were deeply involved in the activities and processes of strategic planning. Soon, five major task forces and other entities were actively involved in the planning process.

In the College Library's "Annual Report" for 1990-91, Mr. DeGennaro notes the importance and the objectives of the strategic planning process. Specifically, the "process was the single

most important activity and accomplishment of the year. The
effort and the results exceeded all expectations. The planning
process had two major objectives. The first was to set clear goals
for the next five years and directions for the next decade and
beyond. The second was to focus the attention of the faculty,
administration, and library staff on the problems and opportunities facing the Library, and to create a climate that would
be hospitable to change and renewal.''[12]

Most of the science libraries did not participate actively in
the College Library's strategic planning process. These libraries
were not organizational units of the College Library. A good
number of the recommendations produced by the task forces
focused on the need for improved services for faculty and students. Eventually, the "gateway concept" surfaced. The Gateway Planning Committee was created to oversee planning for
gateway activities and initiatives. Several gateway task forces
were created to consider specific issues (access and services,
for example). The Gateway Task Force for the Sciences was one
of these task forces. These task forces compiled lists of recommendations. As the issues considered by the Gateway Task
Force for the Sciences were more comprehensive in nature, the
process used to generate recommendations approximated the
process of strategic planning.

RECOMMENDATIONS AND REALITIES
FOR THE FUTURE

The lists of recommendations of the various task forces were
impressive. A significant number of the recommendations have
been seriously considered as realistic options. Several additional
task forces have been created to expedite the implementation
of specific recommendations (user needs assessment, for example). Continued progress is evident.

Nearly 100 recommendations were initially generated by
the Gateway Task Force for the Sciences. The recommendations focused on organizational development and structure,
services for users, and collections. These recommendations were
continually discussed and refined. Currently, there are 28

recommendations. Members of the Task Force included representatives from the Biological Laboratories Library, Botany Libraries, Cabot Science Library, Countway Library of Medicine, Kummel Geological Sciences Library, McKay Applied Sciences Library, Museum of Comparative Zoology Library, Physics Research Library, and the Office of Information Services. The Coordinator of Science/Technology Libraries served as Chair of the Task Force.

The recommendations were numerous and substantial. Nearly 50 percent of the recommendations focused on the important area of services. Nonetheless, the ''process'' used to discuss, deliberate, and compile the recommendations was probably more important than the actual recommendations. In academia, ''process'' tends to underscore (or possibly dominate) life, policy, and procedures. Committees and task forces formulate, reformulate, and assess policy. Some assert that the attention and efforts devoted to committee activities is interminable. Others feel more comfortable with the intense and extensive collegial process. For the Gateway Task Force for the Sciences, the process of collaboration was particularly important.

As the strategic planning process noted above focused on the organizational elements of the College Library, the collaborative efforts of the Gateway Task Force for the Sciences approximated the process of strategic planning for the sciences. This process of discussion, assertion, agreement, disagreement, mediation, and resolution was significant as well as timely. Essentially the process underscored the relative importance of Harvard's science and technology libraries. The relevance of the process was repeatedly noted by individuals in the science/technology libraries and by others within the College Library.

COMMENTS ON THE RECOMMENDATIONS

Dramatic differences in policies and services among the science libraries have been confusing to users. In an attempt to rectify this dilemma, several recommendations have focused on the need to examine and moderate or minimize these differences. The need to be more user-centered underscores all recommendations. User needs feedback and assessment will influence policy and overall direction. As reference and instructional services for all users are valued, the realities of the differences in policies/services will be seriously considered. Some of these unique differences contribute significantly to Harvard's exceptional academic ambiance. Others need to be investigated within the user-centered context and eventually modified.

Electronic access to major databases is essential to effective instructional and research efforts in the sciences. As access to databases such as BIOSIS is not currently provided, several recommendations focus on databases and associated connectivities. These specific recommendations are critical and essentially underlie the potential efficacy of many of the other recommendations. Individually, the science libraries have been unable to provide access to the major databases. Collaboratively, it's possible and likely. An appropriate platform needs to be identified. Effective negotiations, including internal (the libraries) and external (the vendors), are requisites to success. In particular, realistic internal collaborations on the various costs will be essential to success.

The collections have been and will continue to be particularly important. Recommendations focus on the relevance of cooperative collection development and management, preservation priorities, and shared purchases.

A formal ''administrative structure'' needs to be created to coordinate and facilitate. This recommendation is probably somewhat sensitive in nature as a result of the historically decentralized organizational structure. The recommendation focuses on coordination and facilitation, not control. A collective mission for libraries in the sciences is needed. Moreover, the responsibility to cooperate needs to be added to all position descriptions. Representation on relevant policy-related committees and task forces is essential. As a result of the decentralized organizational structure, staff in the sciences feel that they have not been habitually asked to participate on some committees or task forces, and have not been represented. Additionally, creation of a ''Faculty Library Committee for the Sciences'' has been recommended, along with another forum for representation. Such a committee will provide essential faculty assistance and support as well as feedback on specific issues. These recommendations underscore the relevance of coordination, collaboration, facilitation, and organization.

A FOOTNOTE ON THE PROCESS

As noted previously, the concept of trust is important. In a decentralized organizational structure, the degree of total commitment to the realities of collaboration and cooperation is moderated by an occasional lack of trust. With a decentralized tradition of more than 350 years, this is probably normal and needs to be expected. The sensitive balance between tradition and the need to move ahead and consider collaborative alternatives is a realistic element of the planning process.

Coalition management is another essential element of this process. The coalitions are numerous. Effective communication among the various coalitions is critical. Judicious perceptions of the realities and vagaries of the political environment facilitate efforts to move ahead. In *The Fifth Discipline,* Peter Senge discusses the "learning organization." In such an organization, a "climate" is cultivated in which mistakes or errors are essentially valued. Organizational participants learn from their mistakes or errors and then move ahead.[13] Cultivation of this organizational attitude is a requisite to effective coalition management and to collaborative progress. Moreover, in the "learning organization," individuals and, eventually, coalitions are more willing to consider and take risks. If the participants feel that errors and potential failure are, in a sense, valued, they'll be more willing to consider innovative options and take risks.

THE REALIZATION

I started to reflect on ideas for this paper in July and August. The research process commenced in September. I started to write in mid-October. My ideas and reflections have changed and evolved since July/August. We've discussed the concepts

of coordination, cooperation, collaboration, facilitation, and consolidation on numerous occasions. Cooperative instructional
activities, including "model" instructional modules, are being
planned and implemented. Potential organizational collaborations or consolidations will be deliberated in the future. In The
Evolving Educational Mission of the Library, published by
ACRL's Bibliographic Instruction Section (1992), I'm impressed
with the comments and recommendations on the transformation from "bibliographic instruction" to "information literacy."[14] In a sense, this transformation is similar to the
collaborative changes being discussed in the sciences. Within
the context or framework of these discussions and initiatives,
I've realized that the "process" is critically important. While
"process" is frequently criticized in academia, it's particularly
relevant if concepts such as trust are elements of the transformation.

While specific instructional initiatives have not been listed
and described in this presentation, several important proposals
have been planned and implemented, including an electronic
instructional classroom or laboratory. This facility will provide
opportunities to collaborate on instructional activities. The
"trail" of activities and collaborations from mid-1993 to late
February has been one of edification as well as personal and
professional development. Essentially, the various elements of
the "process" have been more important.

These elements need to be deliberated by those in decentralized institutions who are considering or involved in major
organizational or restructuring activities that are underscored
by the importance of interactive instructional methodologies
and techniques. The "forces of change" noted above affect all
collections-based models at all colleges and universities. Instructional activities and initiatives are affected, too, by continuous
changes in the processes of scholarly communication, by pressures to provide immediate access to various forms of information in the sciences, and by less than adequate budgets.
Integration of electronic access options into instructional modules is essential, especially for classes in the sciences. These
options should not be "attached to" the instructional session.

Instead they should be integrated into the general context of the session. Librarians need to work closely with faculty and students to become more familiar with the elements of scholarly communication, including the varied research processes. In doing so they will become full participants in deliberations of relevant instructional and research policies.

CONCLUDING COMMENTS

In relatively large, decentralized institutions, coordination and facilitation are not necessarily simplistic. One needs to be continually aware of the political context or environment as one works with various coalitions to generate and refine a shared vision for the future. Realistic risks are essential to success. Appropriate measures of patience and perseverance facilitate collaborative efforts over time. In particular, respect for the expertise and experiences of all participants is critical. Coalitions and libraries are composed of individuals with differing opinions and numerous suggestions for change or progress. This diversity of opinion is relevant and must be valued and integrated into the shared vision. Additionally, a realization and appreciation of the relevance of the ''process'' is important.

In ''The Future of Bibliographic Instruction and Information Literacy for the Academic Librarian,'' William Miller states that information literacy's future is probably more promising in ''smaller college situations, where librarians have been able to get beyond the superficiality of one-shot lectures and workbooks. . . . ''[15] Moreover, for ''librarians at larger institutions, an alternative path to meaningful information literacy instruction may be through amalgamation with computer centers and other units in a larger teaching (and perhaps administrative) structure.''[16] In this presentation, I've noted and discussed various academic and political realities of an extended process or methodology for the larger, decentralized institution. To move ahead in the 1990s, we'll need to explore all alternative paths.

REFERENCES

1. Rudenstine, Neil R. Letter to the general faculties of Harvard University, 15 October 1993, 1.

2. Rudenstine, Letter, 4.

3. Rudenstine, Neil R. Report to the Board of Overseers (as reported by Harvard University's "Gazette," 29 October 1993, 1).

4. Rudenstine, Report, 1.

5. Rudenstine, Report 10.

6. Dowler, Lawrence. "Gateways to Knowledge: A New Direction for the Harvard College Library," 9.

7. Rosovsky, Henry. The University: An Owner's Manual. New York: W. W. Norton Company, 1990, 32.

8. Rosovsky, The University, 31-32.

9. Reichel, Mary. "Scholarly Communication and Information Needs in 2001: Perceptions of Faculty." Ph.D. diss., Georgia State University, 1992. Also, see Anthony M. Cummings and others, University Libraries and Scholarly Communication, Washington, DC: Association of Research Libraries, 1992.

10. Peters, Paul E. "Leadership Strategies for Networked Organizations." Paper presented at the Harvard College Library, Harvard University, Cambridge, Massachusetts, 12 January 1994.

11. Webster's Third New International Dictionary. Springfield (MA): Merriam-Webster, 1986, 1172.

12. Harvard College Library, "Annual Report 1990-91," 31.

13. Senge, Peter. The Fifth Discipline: The Art and Practice of the Learning Organization. New York: Doubleday, 1990.

14. Baker, Betsy, and Mary Ellen Litzinger, eds. The Evolving Educational Mission of the Library. Chicago: Association of College and Research Libraries, 1992.

15. Miller, William. "The Future of Bibliographic Instruction and Information Literacy for the Academic Librarian." In The Evolving Educational Mission of the Library, edited by Betsy Baker and Mary Ellen Litzinger, 149. Chicago: Association of College and Research Libraries, 1992.

16. Miller, "The Future of Bibliographic Instruction," 149-150.

9

Everyone in the Pool: Staying Afloat with a Good BI Team

Polly P. Frank and Lee-Allison Levene
Memorial Library
Mankato State University

INTRODUCTION

At this conference and in the literature we hear a lot about how we can continue to keep ourselves and our instruction programs up and running while doing more with less. Learning how others address similar problems offers us practical alternatives and stirs us to dig deeper into our own bag of tricks. We can identify the problems but unfortunately we have little control over budget constraints and other external issues. However, we are not without options. To proactively face these budgetary restraints and related issues, our universities challenge us to reevaluate the staffing of our instruction programs. We ask ourselves once again, can anyone else in our libraries and universities help us support our goals?

In this paper we propose a model to attract new members to the team and keep them involved. First examine what kind of staff support we have for our instruction programs at our libraries. We approach other librarians on staff who possess planning, writing, promotional, or technical skills and assess their interest in getting involved in our programs. Find out if our library paraprofessionals and faculty on campus have an interest in our programs. We enlist their help as well. Of course, the dilemma is that even when people support us, we find that support is one thing and involvement is another. How can we convince already overworked librarians, university faculty, and other library staff members to get involved? Furthermore, if our recruitment efforts work, how will we use our colleagues' skills? What will we do to support individual needs? How will we keep them interested in the program?

GETTING THEM IN THE WATER

Support for plans to restructure and build our instruction teams begins with collegial recognition of what we have done in the past and what we are trying to currently accomplish. Our data documents the type, size, and number of BI sessions; college department, and community requests for instruction; and librarian, paraprofessional, and faculty participation in BI. But these records of providing service and attaining goals only show what we can do. To initiate discussion about restructuring we must encourage our colleagues to consider and debate our objectives and the value of the current program. The importance of this step cannot be overstated. From these discussions we assess the support we have from staff to continue responding to current instruction demand. We candidly explain why we need to change what we are doing. Equally important, we also specify how we think restructuring would benefit the instruction program, our current BI staff, and new and future members of the staff. Our administrators and colleagues will encourage us if we not only examine the need but also have valid and persuasive reasons to change. Our rationale may include theoretical or practical points targeting individuals, the whole staff, the needs of the program, and the goals of the library. Here are some arguments we used in the past at MSU:

WHY MORE STAFF INVOLVEMENT IN THE BI PROGRAM?

- Diffuses BI stress early in the term by having others share tasks/classes.
- Commits BI team to share other staff responsibilities later in the term (''payback'' feature).
- Provides a broader base of subject expertise.
- Expands outlook/vision of the team (library public service paraprofessionals and university faculty may offer different perspectives on students' library education needs).
- Increases visibility of staff (out in public view and other PR issues).
- Utilizes staff skills in new applications.
- Maximizes paraprofessional higher level skills and gives them a broader picture of the library.
- Provides teaching and other development opportunities.
- Offers option for flexibility and variety in job responsibilities.
- Builds liaison connections—goes beyond collection development work with a department.
- Builds the library community—the more you work together, the more you build the bond.
- Coteaching helps faculty learn more about library collections /services, become better library advocates, and gain respect for what librarians do and know.
- Coteaching may help librarians learn more about the teaching/learning processes from faculty who have more daily experience in the classroom.
- More staff allows library instructors to become more specialized—teach more classes in areas they know.
- Can be a morale booster for paraprofessionals—identified as having skills needed in program largely dominated by librarians.
- Can help paraprofessionals build relationships with teach-

ing faculty that they may not experience with their regular duties.

These arguments are like a tank suit, one size does NOT fit all. Our rationale for why we need to involve others and why this type of restructuring works depends on each library's mission and instruction program objectives. We do not believe that we are going to convince everyone to jump in the pool and start paddling when we present our arguments. Our initial goal is to convince our administration and staff that our plan to include others has value and merits investigation. We want them to give us the opportunity to examine the feasibility of building our team.

GETTING AND USING NEW HIRES

In gaining approval to explore this concept, we look at who we can involve to ease the stress and keep our programs vital. New hires become potential members of the instruction team. We advocate that all new staff have some instruction or instruction-related responsibilities in their job descriptions. BI staff are not the only ones to benefit from the support. By watching new employees get involved, other librarians and staff see that they will not be left holding the (beach) ball if they come on board and join the instruction team.

The instruction program utilizes whatever instruction-related skills each new hire owns. Some new staff teach while others take on instruction-related assignments. In addition to staff who teach, our programs need people who can work on outreach, advertising, needs assessment, equipment/software installation, program development, and other tasks. New staff may have nonteaching responsibilities simply because our BI programs need help with other assignments. Some may not teach because their jobs have time constraints requiring maximum flexibility in their daily schedule. For example, some staff may need to work oncall with no structured schedule enabling their quick response to crises situations. This might be true for a systems librarian or technician. However successful we are in utilizing new employees skills in some aspect of our program, using new hires only partially addresses our restructuring goals.

ENLISTING CURRENT STAFF

Encouraging other staff and faculty to participate in the instruction program and helping them to recognize the value of this experience presents the biggest challenge. A clear explanation of the scope and extent of the job comes first. Potential instructors not only want these points clarified, they also want to know what they can expect to gain from the experience personally and professionally. The BI staff works together to encourage new membership and to explain the extent of support they provide to their colleagues on the team. Clearly describing the program, targeting potential instructors' needs, and showing collegial support can build interest in participation.

RECRUITING BY BI STAFF

To initiate these restructuring efforts, the instruction coordinator and the head of reference plan as a team. If there are other instruction librarians on staff, the coleaders enlist their help to sell the concept. We explain to the library staff why others should get involved. Collectively introducing our restructuring plan exemplifies the type of teamwork instructors practice in our program. Members of the instruction team recruit others by spelling out how the program works, what we feel students gain, why we participate ourselves, and what kinds of collegial support we get in our work.

EXPLAINING JOB SCOPE

Explaining the scope and extent of the job requires clarity. Instruction team members should simply give the facts and avoid ambiguity.

Be Clear:
New team members will want to know: What guidelines does every member follow? Does the program allow for flexible arrangements?

Work Load:
Instructors want to know exactly what kind of work load they can expect. Can they negotiate a minimum and maximum number of BI assignments with the coordinator?

BI Class Assignments:
In addition, instructors want to know: Can they choose to teach instruction sessions in some subject fields and not others? Can they choose whether or not they will work with lower division, graduate students, or community groups?

Support:
Instructors want to know how much time is allowed for planning? Are faculty required to request sessions ''x'' number of days in advance? What kind of development opportunities will they get: Inservice training? Peer coaching? Continuing education opportunities through other institutions? And certainly, instructors will want to know what kind of clerical support can they expect to receive?

Nonteaching BI Assignments:
Librarians and staff may want to get involved in supporting the program but may not be willing or able to teach. They will want to know: What other type of help is needed in the program? What can they expect in terms of work load and support? (And other pertinent questions from the categories above.)

When instruction librarians, as a team, clarify these points and answer related questions for staff, they exhibit the standard straightforward treatment that all team members can expect to receive.

THE VALUE OF PROGRAM

After explaining the scope and extent of the job, the instruction staff shares their personal views about the program. This is done by outlining examples of what we think instructors gain personally and professionally. Hearing about the value of the program from enthusiastic team members may help new recruits identify with values they share. They may recognize the collegiality and support offered by the team. The instruction librarians ask potential staff to consider, "What's in it for me?" and explain how we try to respond to each instructor's individual needs. When these things happen, our instruction services become programs of attraction rather than promotion.

The list below cites examples of what the MSU BI staff has said about our instruction program. Our comments explain how our involvement in the program benefits us personally and professionally. Your own team members' comments, documented like this and conveyed to other staff, can spark new insight and reinforce shared ideas about your program. Explaining our views about the instruction program, the team reveals that we have diverse reasons to be involved and that every member of the team supports the program. Our team's discerning, enthusiastic, and sincere remarks about the value of the program can favorably influence others who may be considering whether or not they want to be a part of this team. Unique comments of our instruction staff can be regularly updated—a testimony of collective thoughts to help our staff acknowledge and appreciate why we do the work we do. This current list of personal and professional program benefits can help us explain the value of the instruction program to our administrators as well as potential staff.

- Helps me stay on top of new reference sources (when I teach BI classes in that subject area).
- Another opportunity to connect with my liaison departments.
- Sometimes a class just goes well. I get that good feeling that I made the students' lives easier. I made some con-

nection. Nothing else I do as a librarian makes me feel as good as I do then.

- Good sessions give me energy and confidence.
- Great to hang out with the best bunch of librarians—more camaraderie and feeling of being on a team.
- More chance than at Reference desk to teach students how to be independent researchers and library users.
- More chance than at Reference desk to teach students how to evaluate information access and research strategies applied.
- Allows contact with actual library users; my main job (head of collection development) doesn't provide that opportunity often.
- Helps build presentation skills or at least keep them from atrophying.
- Greater opportunity to promote the special collection I develop.
- Forces me simply to bone-up in areas I don't know well and feel more comfortable with them.
- Another "obituary builder" (That is, BI skills are another aspect of public service that I have built into my professional development goals.)
- Opportunity to personally connect and build rapport with faculty and students. I usually don't have that kind of time at the Reference desk.
- Helps me learn more about the whole teaching/learning process and student information needs.

Another recruitment step is taken by talking to nonteaching librarians and staff about their professional values and needs and discussing how we could respond to those needs in our program. When we know what individuals need and value, we find it easier to answer their question, "What's in it for me?" For example, a new instructor may worry about how the new BI classes at the beginning of the quarter will affect her other work. We may find out that this staff member values reliable support and some work reciprocity from her colleagues. Taking action, we have the librarian identify how we can help with her other responsibilities and negotiate to carry out specific assignments later in the term. Here are some examples of how identifying and responding to needs has worked in the past for us.

Value/Need:
Librarian is willing to join team, but wouldn't feel comfortable working with diverse classes; her specialty is health sciences. Also wants to know if she can limit number of classes assigned to her.

Response—Class Assignments in Specialty Area Only:
Identify all classes currently requested in or related to her subject specialty and explain what was covered in the past. Negotiate which classes she will accept and min/max number of classes regularly assigned to her per term.

Value/Need:
Staff members may want to become involved in instruction program but worry about their teaching skills. They want to support the program but want to feel good about whatever involvement they choose.

Response—Offering Options:
Offer a period of ongoing guidance in teaching, open your classrooms for observation, be a peer coach, help co-plan their first term classes, etc. Also, explain other opportunities to help instruction team. Rather than teaching, others may want to work on promotion, advertising, and library guides, etc.

Buoyed Up By Others

When we have librarians modeling the positive nature of a BI program, there exists the realistic possibility of expanding the number of staff involved. Others in the academic setting may be interested in what they see happening in the program and may want to become a part of library instruction. By using a model of attraction, a BI program can entice other librarians, library technicians, and teaching faculty to join the team.

Library Faculty

The strengths of the library instructors can help encourage participation by potential staff. Candidates for the team will not only want to know about their colleagues' individual abilities and expertise, but will also want to know about the support they have to offer. In part, potential staff can recognize the level of collegial support among instructors by seeing how team members interact in their daily activities. However, more evidence of support will be needed. Instruction team candidates will want to know exactly what they can actually count on if they join the team. The spirit that team members display when they talk about instruction can help draw interest in the program as well. Having honest enthusiasm for teaching shows that being involved in the instruction program is a doable thing, not likely to drive new instructors into deep water without a life jacket. Learning about their colleagues' expertise, mutual support, and spirit can help potential instructors recognize what niche they can fill and how they can complement the team.

Here are examples of some of the strengths, skills, support, and other attributes of MSU librarians as described by our colleagues. A team-generated record of an individual staff member's strengths, such as this, could be used to illustrate the support systems for potential team members. The record could also assist team members who want to identify peers who could help them develop specific skills.

Libn A, B & C Models good class planning and offers to help other learn more about how to plan for classes.

Libn D Not afraid to admit to instruction problems, shows us how to ask for help.

Libn E Designs effective images to relay ideas and shares visual aids.

Libn F Works on improving communication with international students in classroom and shares insight gained.

Libn G & H Willing to coteach to offset each other's weak areas.

Libn I Will share examples of various hands-on activities he used to reinforce concepts from lecture. Explains what worked and what didn't work.

Earlier we presented why you might ask your staff to share their own perceptions about the value of the instruction program. We suggested that the real opinions of those librarians actually doing the job might help foster interest in the program among potential staff. In addition, your staff's own description of their team members' strengths and the reliable support system might further encourage others to join the team.

TEACHING FACULTY

Besides the library faculty there are others in the university community we can recruit. We can look to faculty from other departments who have an interest in library instruction that goes beyond having us merely meeting with their class. The librarian can examine the degree of interest and involvement demonstrated by the faculty person when they are co-planning the library session. Some faculty not only talk about how this BI session fits with a library assignment but may want to discuss what reference tools they would like covered or teaching techniques that get a positive response from their class. This is an opportunity for us to explore team-teaching, working together on an assignment sheet, or having the faculty assist with an interactive portion of the BI session. We need to gently probe, testing the direction of their interest and the possibility of greater involvement of faculty with their own classes in library-related instruction.

Another recruiting opportunity comes through examining patterns of BI class requests. For example, in most colleges and universities there are many sections of basic composition, often having library-related assignments. If requests to work with the composition classes are a regularly overwhelming event early in the term, we can consider an alternative approach for dealing with them. Librarians could work with the composition instructors, instead of each class, covering such basics as picking a topic, using the OPAC, searching simple databases, analyzing the results of the search, and locating the articles. The composition instructor, in turn, can teach these basics to their classes as the students begin working with a composition assignment. To help this occur, we can go beyond providing librarian expertise to teach the teachers. We may also provide resources, such as a classroom with connections to an online catalog or a CD-ROM unit with sample discs. By providing facilities, reference sources, and librarian expertise we can manage the number of bibliographic sessions that we teach and eliminate being overwhelmed with many early-in-term class requests. We can offer our assistance for more advanced instruction with those classes later in the term. Expanding the BI team to include the composition instructors helps us address our immediate needs.

While many BI sessions take place during the usual class time of the 50-minute hour, some may be scheduled for two hours, three hours, or more. These extended classes, whether for university students or regional high school groups, present another opportunity to draw outside instructors into the BI team. For example, if a portion of the BI session includes some time on task in the library, participation by the classroom instructor can be critical. Both the librarian and the classroom instructor can assist students while they search library resources to complete their assignment. Without the instructor being present, we would need to assign another librarian the task of assisting us in working with the student.

Identifying individuals interested in BI who can help us and situations where BI can be streamlined are effective methods to keep our team afloat.

LIBRARY PARAPROFESSIONALS

Within every library there are untapped groups that have valuable skills to offer to a BI program. One such group is the library paraprofessionals. At MSU, one technician with a geography degree regularly teaches library instructional sessions for geography students. Her understanding of the discipline and in-depth knowledge of several map CD-ROMs gives her unique qualifications for teaching these sessions. This person wants to be involved because she can present a positive image of the library as well as have the intrinsic reward of knowing she is helping students. Another technician has a Spanish degree, as well as mastery of our OPAC, making him a candidate for working with Spanish-speaking groups. Both of these paraprofessionals feel they are contributing to the mission of the library by assisting in providing BI services.

Once again, a program of attraction is preferable when building your team. We look at the strengths available, then approach selected library paraprofessionals. We tell them why we are interested in having them become a part of the pool, indicate what kind of developmental/training support they can expect, and, if they are interested, pair them with a librarian who can encourage and expand their teaching skills. There is the potential for increased utilization of library paraprofessionals in BI, with administrative support for this. This group, like the librarians, needs staff development and training in order to be effective with their teaching. The keys are finding out the education, training, and special skills the paraprofessionals have, discerning those who would truly enjoy a role in instruction, and assessing administrative and paraprofessionals' supervisor support.

OTHER LIBRARY FACULTY

Within any library there are also librarians who do not teach, may not feel comfortable with the idea of teaching, or may simply choose not to teach. However, these librarians may have skills that are valuable to instruction and getting them involved in the non-teaching portion of the BI program is important. Many instruction programs are responsible for or have a part in working on library pathfinders and handouts, new library technology publicity, library display cases, or university special events. Even though their liaison work and collection development can include some amount of teaching, librarians might not view this work as "instruction" in the formal sense. There is an "instructional" element to all of these efforts, although none require someone to stand up and teach. Inviting and involving those individuals who write clearly , understand technology, or can organize information offers the op-

portunity of expanding the BI team and forging new relationships. A joint project, such as planning BI publicity, offers an
opportunity for the instruction librarians and the non-teaching
librarian to learn from one another.

ADMINISTRATORS

Residing on the periphery, yet vital to any bibliographic instruction program, is library administration. Unlike library
paraprofessionals, non-teaching librarians, or faculty and teaching assistants from other departments, administrators may not
be an active part of the BI team. However, they do play a key
role in our programs. It is crucial to any lively program that
we keep our administration educated about BI If our administration understands the goals, as well as the process, of our
program we are more likely to get the needed support. For example, we mentioned earlier the concept of having a BI component in the job description of all new library hires. Getting
this type of support from administration gives a message to the
library staff about the priority of BI in the library mission. Additionally, our administration, if educated about your instruction program, will understand the importance of supporting
the need for classroom materials, scheduling flexibility, improved equipment, continuing education, and clerical assistance.

DIFFERENT STROKES

Given the diversity of personalities, skills, and commitments
of individuals who may be drawn onto the team, those guiding BI cannot afford to have uniform expectations of all who
are involved. Leaders, as well as BI colleagues, need to be flexible and inviting to all comers. Without this we risk losing potential instructors even before we have gotten them involved in
our program.

Having a BI coordinator or team leader helps in the implementation of the model under consideration. This 'point per-

son' keeps BI afloat through instructor education, coordinated teaching assignments, idea filtering, and group leadership. The coordinator models using attraction to draw in additional instructors through his or her leadership of the program.

No matter how encouraging and inviting the coordinator and instruction staff are, there are always staff that can't or won't teach. However, all is not lost. Although library tours for the disoriented student and staff fall under the auspices of many BI programs, some library staff do not consider this 'teaching.' Instead they look upon tours as a 'safe' activity and are willing to get involved. Drop-in demonstrations of the online catalog or CD-ROMs may be more challenging for some, but still have the aura of a non-threatening BI activity. Staff may need to see what is typically demonstrated at these sessions before they choose to get involved. We have found that other staff usually can be convinced that they are capable of handling this BI activity. Additionally, when new services or technologies change our environment, we need skilled writers to advertise this to our users or provide written instructions on 'how to use it.' Individuals or teams can be approached by the BI coordinator to do this, diffusing the total burden of these responsibilities from the regular BI librarians.

Listening to teaching likes and dislikes voiced by BI team members, such as "I would rather swim in shark-infested waters than give a BI session to legislative history classes," is important. One method of discerning a BI instructor's preferences is through a survey which will help identify their teaching strengths and dreaded subject areas.

Beyond this, our BI coordinator has to develop a sense of the personalities involved—both the library instructors and the requesting faculty. We do not want to pair a faculty person, who is a tightly structured planner, with a high energy, go-with-the-flow BI librarian. The coordinator tries to avoid mismatches with the teaching faculty and library instructor. Over time, our coordinator will know which librarians are the punters and who can step in for a sick BI librarian, who to pair with whom for peer coaching in the classroom, which individuals enjoy teaching high school groups, and which individuals enjoy taking on many classes each week early in the term and being free from this pressure later in the term (also called high density teaching).

The information that the coordinator gleans from working with the cadre of instruction librarians and staff, such as their strengths, stylistic differences, discipline interests, and so forth, can lead to the formation of teams within the library. These teams, or sub-groups, can work on a variety of projects central to BI By matching people's long suits, some may work on BI program guidelines, while others may be more interested in developing library publications or advertising.

THE WORKOUT
(KEEPING THE TEAM AFLOAT
WHILE WE GO THE DISTANCE)

Individual lasting power in the program depends on individual and collective support. The responsibility for helping team members keep their heads above water and experience success in their efforts belongs to us all. Each team player serves some aspect of this function. Our responsibilities for instructors' and other team members' success vary but our goal is the same. We want our program to succeed and we want our players to benefit from their involvement.

HELP FROM ADMINISTRATORS

Evidence of library administrators' concern for the individual success of team members largely comes from their continuing response to requests for programmatic needs. In addition, administrators can greatly enhance the success of the program by expressing their support and campaigning for the program on campus. Administrators can encourage individual instructors by acknowledging faculty thank you letters they receive regarding a librarian's good work. Commitment to the program by members of the team may grow if they can witness the active endorsement of our library administrators for the program and encouragement of the individuals involved.

HELP FROM COORDINATOR

Our instruction coordinators also help keep instructors and other team members "swimming." Coordinators must negotiate with administrators for programmatic concerns and attend to the individual needs of team members as well. To help individuals succeed, our coordinators must adhere to the plan that was jointly negotiated with each individual. They should regularly review that plan to confirm that all commitments have been met. This is all part and parcel of attracting and keeping good instructors. By honoring this information, our coordinator builds trust in the program and the process. In addition, coordinators must listen attentively to each individual's concerns and respond to problems that arise. Coordinators can help encourage participants by avoiding "favorite team member" status and regularly applauding and celebrating the work of individuals and the group. A good rule of thumb is to use kudos as if they were cash. That is, when a faculty member commends a librarian's good work, coordinators should forward their letters to persons on campus who affect promotion and tenure decisions such as personnel committees, campus appointment groups, and university administrators. By keeping classroom equipment up and running and coordinating clerical support for instructors, instruction coordinators go a long way to help make our team function smoothly. Participating in the program as instructors, coordinators model collegial involvement and experience the front line concerns. By networking with other coordinators, they learn other ways to address these concerns and keep team members involved.

HELP FROM OUR COWORKERS

The support of instruction colleagues probably does more to nurture and retain team membership than any other single factor. Instruction team members offer assistance in a variety of ways. Sharing our knowledge, time and "trade secrets," we not only make life easier for our colleagues but also model how to be team players. Our willingness to accept our share of BI assignments, cover reference hours scheduled during BI sessions, offer guidance in class planning, assist with active learning sessions, share materials developed for related sessions, and countless other examples of support, reveals the kind of cooperative spirit we value. Team members serve as mentors, peers, and sometimes even counselors. We demonstrate how to plan classes and teach effectively, how to be team players, and equally important, how to stay alive in the process.

HELPING OURSELVES

All team members must also take responsibility for our own well-being in the program. If we don't know, we can learn from our colleagues how to build endurance so we can ''go the distance'' without killing ourselves. We can learn how to ask for help, try new ways of doing things, set limits (and stick to them!), and request time off when needed.

Often times instructors will avoid asking for help because we think we SHOULD be able to handle the workload or other instruction related problems. The result is that we focus on what is wrong instead of what is right and as a consequence, delay taking action to make it better. To get help, team members can contact a trusted coworker or the instruction coordinator to share ideas and concerns. Together, we can work on practical problems, vent frustrations, or simply learn how our colleagues tackle similar pressures.

Another way instruction team members can take responsibility for our own well-being is to acknowledge our own part in doing ourselves in. Superhuman agendas, unchecked perfectionist streaks, the inability to say no, and trying to prove oneself to others are just a few of the traits that undermine the instructors' ability to succeed. Instruction team members must be able to identify our own limits and stand firm on what we have chosen not to do. Also, instructors may need to request a timeout period or ''mini-sabbatical'' for a term when they can anticipate added personal or professional obligations. Setting limits helps the team member live in the solution rather than in the problem.

We will take ownership in the instruction program when we practice these principles and when we see our administrators, coordinator, and colleagues work together to keep us involved in the program. When there is evidence of continuing administrative support, respect for individually negotiated plans, and help offered by colleagues, BI ownership in the program grows.

CONCLUSION

The pairing of two significant pressures, the demand for instruction services and academic downsizing, creates a fiscal milieu that could drown some library programs. We cannot control the external restraints imposed upon us. However, the model presented in this paper is designed to keep bibliographic instruction swimming along by addressing issues that librarians can influence or control. This model is one of attraction, creating a broader base for an instruction program by using more library staff and teaching faculty. By enlisting the help of BI instructors to expand the base of instructors, recruiting staff to work on other BI tasks, capitalizing on individual instructors' strengths, garnering administrative understanding and support, and tailoring support to meet each librarian's needs, we can keep BI afloat and vital in this time of fiscal turbulence.

10

Teaching Future Librarians to Teach

Esther Grassian and Joan Kaplowitz
University of California at Los Angeles

Does the expression "more with less" sound familiar to you? What is this more that we are doing with less? In many cases, I suspect it has something to do with instruction. But even if it is not directly related to instruction, more with less means stretching our staff's time thinner and thinner. With just so many hours in the day, the net result is we each have less time to devote to whatever we have to do—instruction included.

Instruction, especially anything new, is one of the most labor-intensive things we do. Terry Smith, in his book *Making Successful Presentations*, estimates that it takes one hour of preparation time for each minute that we actually are presenting. Designing point of use pieces, pathfinders and online system help screens are equally time-consuming. Plus we need to factor in the "learning how to do it" time.

Somewhere along the line we each have to learn these "how-to" skills - how to do needs assessments, how to select modes of instructions, how to develop new instruction, design materials, and evaluate the program. Not to mention learning how to stand up in front of a group and make an effective presentation. The way we acquire these skills can mean the difference between hours or days, perhaps even weeks of work.

A librarian who has not had systematic training either through library school or independent courses or workshops is forced to go through the sometimes painful and always time-consuming process of learning what works and what doesn't with a heavy reliance on the trial and error method of learning.

If you are lucky enough to have a co-worker or supervisor with the requisite skills who is willing (and has the time to) share his or her expertise, this one-on-one training, while more efficient than doing it alone, may be nearly as time-consuming when you consider that each hour of training is really two hours of staff time, the learner's and the trainer's.

A formal course such as the one we teach has much to offer. First, the material is presented in a systematic, organized fashion which links theory to practice. Instead of people learning one at a time, we have groups of 20-30 people developing a base level of skills all at once. The time savings is phenomenal. Imagine, you had ten people who all needed to learn how to build a building and it took ten hours to acquire this knowledge. If each person is learning on his or her own, it takes 10 x 10 hours of learning or 100 hours. If these same ten people are learning in a group, it only takes 1 x 10 hours or 10 hours total.

So, now that I have convinced you that a course is a good idea, Esther will talk about what you need to know in order to teach.

Questions for audience:

1. How many of you have ever given a BI lecture, participated in a workbook program, or prepared some sort of instructional material for your users?
2. How many of you have learned about BI through workshops, on the job training or from your colleagues?
3. How many have taken a BI course in library school?
4. How many wished you had?

I asked these questions of the audience at a CCLI California Library Association Conference program in 1991, when Joan and I first gave a presentation on this course. Most had done BI and had learned about it outside of library school. Just one or two of the 100 or so people there had taken a BI course. They all wished they had, and had some definite ideas about what they thought BI librarians should have learned in library school.

Does anyone here today remember going to that program?

It is now three years later. We have all been experiencing the joys and terrors of a warp-speed technological "ride." Have our thoughts changed? What is our reaction now to the question: "What should BI librarians learn in library school?"

In a minute, I would like you to raise your hands and give me your answers to this question. I will write down your answers on for everyone to see. When we have gotten a number of responses, I will ask you to vote for your favorite answers, and we will come up with a list of your top five responses. Then I will show you the top answers we got in 1991 and the top proficiencies identified in a 1989 BIS survey and reported in the March 1993 College & Research Libraries article by Diana Shonrock and Craig Mulder. ("Instruction Librarians: Acquiring the Proficiencies Critical to Their Work." College & Research Libraries 54(2):137-49)

What are your answers?

The top answers from 1991 were:

1. Instructional Ability
2. Communication Skills
3. Cognitive Styles/Learning Theory (tied with following item)
3. Handout/instructional material design
4. Value/use of media/technology in reinforcing communication
4. Research and evaluation methodologies

The top five of the 25 proficiencies listed in the Mulder & Shonrock article are:

1. Administrative Ability
2. Communication Skills
3. Evaluate the Overall Effectiveness of the Program
4. Goals and Objectives
5. Instructional Ability

Joan will now discuss what we decided to include in our course.

The course outline we gave out gives you a pretty good idea of what topics we finally settled on for the class. Getting there was a long and difficult process. Like all BI librarians we wanted to present more than we had time for. So we prioritized, anguished, cut, anguished some more, and finally came up with some basic notions about what the bottom-line was for what to include.

They are things like:

1. What is BI and why do we do it? This is basically a review of the underlying philosophy of the field.
2. An historical perspective or where did today's BI come from? This is Esther's specialty.
3. An introduction to Educational Psychology especially in the areas of the Psychology of Learning and Cognitive Styles. This one is my portion of the course.
4. The steps involved in planning, administrating, developing and evaluating a BI program.
5. An introduction to and practice in presentation skills and classroom management.
6. Consciousness-raising on what are current problems, challenges and controversies in BI today. This of course varies from year to year.

So we had the what. Next came the how. How to present this material? And this is where we made our biggest mistakes. The first time we taught the course we so wanted to share all we knew and all we had been through to get there that we dominated the class. We talked at them and although we said we wanted them to ask questions and make comments, there was rarely any time for them to do so.

Worse yet, we required them to turn in reading reports on a variety of issues or topics over the course of the quarter. We thought it was a way of letting them make their opinions known to us. They thought it was punitive and a way for us to make sure they were doing the readings.

So on round two or the second incarnation of the course,

no more reading reports and less teacher-centered instruction. We made every attempt to talk less and listen more. The reading reports were replaced by student-led group discussions on the same sort of issues and controversies that had been the topics of the reading reports. Groups of four to six students run the class for the first hour of the session. The instructor listens, takes notes and keeps her mouth shut. Until after the break that is, when she responds and reacts to the previous discussion. It's a wonderfully stimulating and energizing experience for all concerned. You never really know what to expect so it really keeps the instructor on her toes.

A second major change from round one to round two was the way we handled the major course requirement which is a written proposal for the development of a new BI project. Our first class complained they did not have enough experience to do this and were dissatisfied with the feedback they received. So we turned the paper into a kind of role-playing exercise. The project was developed in stages starting with a memo to an administrator and getting longer and more detailed as the course progressed. We played the role of the administrator who had to be convinced this was a good idea. The administrator (us) responded in writing at each step with questions, comments, and concerns. Just like real life. Again this proved to be enormously successful and much more enjoyable for all concerned.

Esther taught round three and continued to make these kinds of student-responsive changes. She added a brainstorming exercise as a means of solving a real-life instructional problem, and the ''The One-Minute Paper'' as a feedback mechanism at the end of each session and as a follow-up and way to generate more discussion at the beginning of the next one. She also solicited new real-life instructional problems for students' final projects, and made very effective use of e-mail as a way to promote and continue discussion. I am scheduled to teach round four starting in April 1994 and plan to try a new technique for grading the group discussions. Each member of the facilitating group will be responsible for grading the contributions of every other member of that group and reporting these grades to me. Hopefully this will provide a better mechanism for determining the individual student's contribution to the group process. All of these changes reflect what I believe has become our underlying philosophy of education which we present at the very first class meeting of the course. It's then that we emphasize the notion that learning is a shared responsibility. We will make the material available and give them every opportunity to learn it. But they have to do the work. They will get as much out of the course as they are willing to put into it. And the harder each person works the greater benefit for everyone. The course has really evolved from a teacher-centered view of the students as tabular rasas waiting to be enlightened by our expert knowledge to a student-driven course based on the principle of self-directed learning. Just goes to show you that we too are capable of learning.

Now let me turn it over to Esther for a glimpse into the future.

What does the future hold for GSLIS 426, as the UCLA library school has been merged with the School of Education and has itself been downsized? Twenty courses have been cut from the program and admissions have been cut from 100 per year to 60 per year. Marcia Bates, Faculty Chair and tireless champion of the School, has said that 426 is an extremely important course, and that she has recommended to the faculty that it be offered every year, unlike most electives, which will be offered every other year.

Since this decision is out of our hands, we have been focusing on the course content and structure instead, and plan to try many exciting ideas whenever we have a chance to teach the course again.

> We will try to capitalize on our new relationship with the School of Education by establishing some sort of permanent relationship with the School's Teacher Education Laboratory, the center for student teacher training.

> In 1993, the cutting edge BI issue was teaching the Internet. We see more coverage of such new challenges to BI as the Internet develops and as we see the introduction of software like Mosaic, for example.

> Each year we invite line librarians from various types of library settings to come and speak to the class in a panel. We are now

planning to have panelists who will reflect the "new tradition" BI—e.g., teaching "the library without walls" as well as the "old tradition"—e.g., course-integrated one-shot lectures.

How many of you use e-mail? As e-mail has become more and more a vital part of our professional lives, we plan to increase its use for class assignments and questions based on the readings. We also plan to continue asking students to subscribe to BI-L, to keep abreast of to the minute critical issues concerning BI librarians

The challenging effects of downsizing will be with us for a very long time to come. We have presented you with some thoughts on how a course like this can prepare new librarians for a whole range of teaching and training responsibilities.

Fewer than a dozen library schools in the U.S. and Canada offer a full-credit BI course. UCLA GSLIS is at the cutting edge in offering this course. At a 1991 ALISE/BIS program which I moderated, Herb White said that BI courses would not be offered widely in library schools until employers requested it in job postings. This is what I said to the CLA audience in 1991, and I can only repeat it for you today:

It is time to let Herb White and library schools know that BI coursework is not only important—it is essential. It is time to start adding phrases to our job postings like 'BI coursework would highly benefit applicants.' It is time to stop wishing and hoping. It is time to start doing.

11

BI and Collaborative Learning: A Partnership in Library Literacy

Michele G. Hanson
University of Arizona

One objective of the librarian who teaches—whether in a classroom, at a library orientation, or at the reference desk—is for the user to become more self-sufficient. The image this conjures up, for most of us, is that of an independent researcher who approaches the librarian occasionally with thorny problems, but is otherwise able to manage on his or her own. Reading, writing, class assignments or publications—all are done alone.

What if we took a different slant on this research process? imagine instead three or four students clustered around a CD-ROM terminal in the reference area after a BI session with their class. One of them is having trouble with the concept of Boolean searching, but the others are explaining as they go. One person remembers the librarian explaining how to use the thesaurus, and suggests they try to find more appropriate search

terms. When they do need help, say with limiting by publication year, the librarian at the reference desk is able to teach
several students at one time. The students divide up the citations on the print-out; each will read one or two articles and
summarize for the group at their next meeting. These students,
too, are learning to be "self-sufficient," but they are doing so
as part of a community, by learning collaboratively.

The concept of collaborative learning encompasses many
different pedagogical techniques.

1. a long-term research or study group
2. a task force that meets intensely for a month to propose
   solutions to a problem
3. writing workshops that change every class period
4. brainstorming activities; and students pairing up after a
   twenty-minute lecture to review its content

In short, collaborative learning situations are as varied as
the people involved with them. Whereas the instructor serves
as the voice of authority in the traditional model of education,
collaborative learning methods invite students to enter into a
dialogue. Whatever the form it takes, collaborative learning "actively involves participants in their own learning" (Trimbur 87)
by providing a forum where they are engaged with the content, the process, and each other.

More and more librarians are incorporating collaborative
learning techniques into their instruction sessions, for a variety of reasons. One is that in these times of limited resources—
both human and material—it is expedient to have students share
computer terminals, print indexes, and the librarians' time and
effort. As class sizes grow and information technology becomes
more varied, instructors are not able to spend as much time
with individuals as they would like; in collaborative learning
situations.

However, students provide and receive that individual attention by helping each other.

The benefits to learning collaboratively are far greater than
simply sharing resources. This can range from the potential for
a more lively classroom to studies showing that collaborative

learning "results in higher achievement, more positive relationships among students, and healthier psychological adjustments than does competitive or individualistic learning" (Johnson, Johnson and Smith 1). Although collaborative learning methods have been advocated as early as the late nineteenth century, particularly in composition classes (Gere 16), and brought to the fore in the 1970s, they have been slow to catch on in "that last bastion of hierarchy and individualism, the American college classroom" (Bruffee, "Conversation" 646).

In recent years, however, there has been growing interest across the disciplines. In rhetoric and composition, for example, Donald Stewart notes in a 1988 article that a "major ideological shift is underway" (58). In education, Johnson, Johnson and Smith say that "we are entering an era of interdependence and mutuality" (1); and Jean MacGregor asserts that "[a]s the 1990s begin, interest in collaborative learning has probably never been greater" (21).

In the field of library science, Jean Sheridan makes the case that collaborative learning is appropriate for library instruction for several reasons: it "recognizes the importance of affective environmental elements, such as comfort in the environment, acceptance, and absence of fear" ("Reflective" 26); it is part of a "holistic, or connected education"; and it places more emphasis on the process of research (23). In their article, "Bibliographic Instruction and Collaborative Learning," Marjorie Warmkessel and Frances Carothers suggest that "CL may be an effective means of achieving integration" of bibliographic instruction with the requirements of a course, and describe an experience using the technique of "pairing" to instruct an education class in using the ERIC CD-ROM (5).

These latter publications imply that a growing number of librarians are aware of and practicing collaborative learning methods. In December of 1993, I posted a notice on the BI Listserv asking for people to share their experiences using collaborative learning, and received over 20 responses, nearly all enthusiastic. Librarians across the country suggested a variety of reasons why they use such techniques. Sharyl McMillian-Nelson (University of Missouri-Kansas City), for example, says that "students are much less likely to be bored if they are doing a good portion of the talking and teaching. It also makes each class a new experience for me. . . . We can discuss what they want to know, rather than what I think they want to know." Alice DeCristoforo of Indiana University of Pennsylvania says this:

> We enjoyed the collaborative teaching and the students enjoyed working together in groups. Evaluation forms were filled out after the class with most responding very positively to the group experience. They found it less stressful because they shared the responsibility of learning something new in a much more informal setting. The informality of the process made it easier for them to ask each other questions and discuss answers as they examined sources. They were much more actively involved in the learning process and discovered that they could be teachers as well as learners.

Kenneth Bruffee, one of the most recognized names in the latter discipline, makes a good case for learning more about theory:

> Sometimes collaborative learning works beyond my highest expectations. Sometimes it doesn't work at all. Recently, though, I think I have been more successful. The reason for that increased success seems to be that I know a little more now than I did in the past about the complex ideas that lie behind collaborative learning. ("Conversation" 636)

Jean Sheridan has explored the research going on in education and describes a number of applications for bibliographic instruction ("Rethinking Andragogy," "The Reflective Librarian"). I should like to turn to some of the theoretical discussions in rhetoric and composition, not only because it is rich and valuable, but also because of the often close ties between English departments and the library. Students in composition classes read not only fiction and poetry, but the literature from many other fields, and this interdisciplinary approach lends itself well to students participating in heterogeneous groups. Writing groups— students providing each other feedback to revise drafts, a kind of collaboration—have been a methodology for some writing instructors since the early 1800s, but have gained more attention since the 1970s (Gere 29). Moreover, composition students are often assigned research papers, and may even be required to complete a library skills and research component of the course.

Kenneth Bruffee bases his collaborative learning theories on social constructionist epistemology, which "assumes that entities normally called reality, knowledge, thought, facts, selves and so on are constructs created by communities of like-minded peers" ("Social Construction" 774). In his essay, "Collaborative Learning and the 'Conversation of Mankind'," Bruffee makes the case that "human conversation takes place within us as well as among us, and that conversation as it takes place within us is what we call reflective thought" (639). This "conversation," then, is both internal and external, and reflective thought and social conversation are interdependent: since "thought is internal conversation, thought and conversation tend to work largely in the same way" (639).

Bruffee quotes the poet Michael Oakeshott when he writes, "We first experience and learn 'the skill and partnership of conversation' in the external arena of direct social exchange with other people" (639).

Understanding our thought processes requires a sense of our community and our place within that community. By developing our abilities to work in a community, we expand our thinking skills; as Bruffee says, "To think well as individuals we must learn to think well collectively" (640).

Linda Flower, another rhetorician, has in common with Bruffee the belief that the complexity of one's thought is challenged and improved through interaction and negotiation with others. Discussing the attributes of "inner speech" in adults, she borrows from Jean Piaget and Lev Vygotsky's studies of the developing thought of children. Both men observed in children an "egocentric" speech that "made no concessions to the needs of the listener" (271). Similarly, Flower identifies in adult writers a stage that she calls "Writer-Based prose," which does not recognize the needs of a reader. Such writing is characterized by various "symptoms," including "unfocused and apparently pointless discussion," underdeveloped ideas, and scenarios meaningful to the writer, but not so conveyed to the reader (269). Skillful writers are able to move from Writer-Based to Reader-Based prose. "The transformations that produce Reader-Based writing," Flower says, "include these: Selecting a focus of mutual interest to both reader and writer. Moving from facts, scenarios and details to concepts . . . [and creating] a rhetorical structure built on the logical and hierarchical relationships between ideas." (292)

In essence, while Writer-Based prose provides a wealth of material for early drafts, the writer must eventually recognize that writing is not merely solipsistic expression, but that it becomes part of a social relationship. Both reader and writer have a responsibility to each other; the writer takes into account the audience's need for pertinent information, a unifying purpose, and logical organization, while the reader tacitly agrees to pay close attention to the writer's form and content. Neither role is passive; it is indeed a partnership.

ENCOURAGING PARTNERSHIPS

I would like to consider how Bruffee's metaphor of conversation might apply to libraries, which I think of as loci of a number of long, complex human conversations that have shifted from papyrus scrolls to books and serials, to computer databases and interactive media. This "conversation"—which implies the active participation of everyone involved—is to be encouraged among our students. We might ask, What sort of community is created in our libraries? For example ,in the reference area at the University of Arizona, the noisiest students are, not surprisingly, graduate students from the library school, who primarily get together to learn the sources for their reference classes. The reference area becomes their laboratory. But what about other students? Do they have access to group study rooms? Are they encouraged by their professors to work together, or does informal learning take place as they "socialize" in the library's study areas? Do librarians encourage the "conversation" Bruffee talks about, or do we actually discourage any collaboration among undergraduates? Students completing library skills workbooks, for example, may be penalized for having the same answers; we call that cheating. I raise these questions not to suggest that collaborative learning become the whole of our pedagogical approach to bibliographic instruction, but that we consider various ways its implementation would be appropriate. Some fields have been more open to collaboration than others. The humanities, for example, have traditionally been reluctant to entertain alternatives to the archetype of the lone researcher, but in the sciences, collaboration is the norm for several reasons. Linda Ede and Andrea Lunsford, researching collaborative learning and writing in various scientific and technological professions, confirm that "the technological complexity of research, the nature of funding (which encourages large research teams), and the increase in interdisciplinary research simply mandate collaboration" (74).

The trend is seen not only in the sciences, but in other fields as well. Ede and Lunsford studied seven professional associations, including the American Institute of Chemists, the APA, the International City Management Association, and the MLA, and found that collaborative writing is "a fact of life" (72). The authors "were struck . . . by the number of people who listed 'ability to work well with others' as the most important factor in their fields" (66).

Librarians themselves are well aware of the necessity and benefits of working collaboratively, as we see in our many committees, conferences, and listservs. We may find it appropriate to expand these professional models, not only in our relationships with students, but also with faculty. Warmkessel and Carothers, for example, call for greater collaboration between the librarian and classroom instructor and a "strong collegial relationship," where "mutual cooperation, support, and understanding are essential" (5).

ENABLING STUDENTS TO WORK COLLABORATIVELY

Collaborative learning requires that the instructor share with students the responsibility of shaping the educational experience. Consequently, the instructor must relinquish some control. This can be disconcerting for those who want to know exactly what to expect before it happens. Fortunately planning, a willingness to be flexible, and practice (perhaps even some luck)will lead to success. "It is," says John Dewey, "a much more difficult task to work out the kinds of materials, of methods, and of social relationships that are appropriate to the new education than is the case with traditional [i.e., lecture-based] education" (29). One can't expect simply to group students together and hope something happens without any preparation. Many students have not had experience working together, but are in fact used to a more competitive environment, or, perhaps more commonly, one in which they don't have to do anything but listen and take notes.

In their book, Cooperative Learning: Increasing College Faculty Productivity, Johnson, Johnson, and Smith describe several elements that are key to effective sessions. The first, called "positive interdependence," basically asks students to share resources. As Alice DeCristoforo puts it, she and her colleague Lora Mirza found that "we could encourage more group interaction if [students] had to share the exercise packets instead of each one receiving their own copy."

DeCristoforo describes a class activity that illustrates positive interdependence: for an English 102 class working on a major term paper, the assignment was based on a search strategy, with the whole class working on the same topic but groups working on separate components—encyclopedias, online catalog, periodical indexes (print and computer). . . . Each group had an information and exercise sheet dealing with the particular resource they were examining. After the groups finished their work, the class would reconvene and each group would present their resource to the whole class. It was like bringing the pieces of a puzzle together so that we could see how they fit to form a whole picture.

The sharing of resources leads to "promotive interaction; that is, individuals encouraging and facilitating each other's efforts to achieve" (Johnson, Johnson and Smith 18). This element of effective collaborative learning involves group discussion, performance, and feedback for improvement. Assigning "roles" is one way to foster this promotive interaction.

Imagine, for example, a session involving ERIC on CD-ROM, where the instructor first introduces the concepts of a database, Boolean searching, and the thesaurus. When the groups clustered around a CD-ROM are ready to experiment, they assign themselves the roles of typist, recorder, facilitator, and checker. Their goal is to find materials relating to the development of multidisciplinary textbooks for primary grades. During the discussion of the appropriate terms to use, the "recorder" takes notes on suggestions for possible search strategies, and the "facilitator" in the group makes sure everyone agrees before the "typist" enters the search string.

Periodically, the "checker" asks "every member of the group to explain what is being learned" (Johnson, Johnson, Smith 63). In this way, the concepts introduced at the beginning of the session are reinforced through application and review; in addition, every member of the group becomes responsible for the group's success.

Another technique that promotes interaction, suggested by Bruce Sajdak (Neilson Library, Smith College), challenges students to problem-solve. Small groups develop a sample CD-ROM search with no instruction. Then an actual group's search (or more if time permits) gets used as a real-life example of what works and doesn't work as the librarian performs the search as the group designed it on a projected CD-ROM. Then other groups get a chance to give feedback on how to fix the inevitable mistakes. Not only does this exercise engage individuals in their small groups, the whole class is brought back together to share their findings.

The collaborative learning situation may open the way to potential controversy. Conflict is an understandable result when people with different perspectives, information, and experiences interact. Students may be encouraged to reach an agreement, but this is not always possible or even desirable. Joseph Trimbur, discussing the criticism that social construction's emphasis on group consensus may ultimately lead to conformity and "group think," argues that "consensus cannot be known without its opposite—without the other voices at the periphery of the conversation" (608). Peter Elbow, an important figure in the move toward teaching writing as a process, asks us to "break out of [the] habit'' of always wanting to come to agreement: ''Only by inhibiting the compulsive urge to settle things can you bring out the maximum differences'' and encourage diversity of thought (111).

Recognizing these other voices—indeed, recognizing that some voices remain silent—can be difficult. It is much easier simply to lecture; then others don't have an opportunity to challenge us. Controversy can be positive, for it ''promotes uncertainty about the correctness of one's views, an active search for more information, a reconceptualization of one's knowledge and conclusions, and, consequently, greater mastery and retention of the material being discussed'' (Johnson, Johnson and Smith 33). Controversy may make us uncomfortable, but if instructor and students alike are to understand ourselves, our knowledge communities, and discourse communities, we need to allow these other voices to be heard.

Another potential problem raised by conferring authority to students is that they might refuse to accept it. Explaining the purpose of this methodology may help them to understand why their participation is important for everyone involved. In addition, some measures may be taken to make students accountable for their participation. In a situation where students are graded on their efforts, a process for peer- and self-evaluation may be developed. (See Wiener, e.g.) Since librarians seldom grade, however, the following strategies may be more useful for helping students keep focused: moving among the small groups so that students are aware of your presence; listening to their discussions; prompting them or asking questions if the group seems to have stalled; and letting them know that individuals will be chosen at random to report to the whole class what the small group has accomplished. In addition, students may be asked to complete a brief evaluation at the end of the session, not only to provide the librarian with valuable feedback, but also to reflect on their individual contributions.

As students learn to question their own and each others' assumptions, they may also be encouraged to analyze those of the texts they read. Students tend to approach the printed word as static, and do not attempt to interpret the context of a piece of writing or the validity of its claims. The active engagement with a text may be promoted by asking small groups to compare two texts—one from a scholarly journal, another from a more popular magazine—about a similar topic. How do they differ in language? Research techniques? What do you know about the authors? What biases might they have? In this way, students may see the texts as an invitation to conversation rather than the final word.

CONCLUSION

As librarians, we are at least tangentially concerned with the education of every student who makes use of the library's resources. Our desire to provide students with tools for lifelong learning should include collaborative learning. It is not a panacea, as Stewart reminds us, but "it should become yet one more resource" (80), one whose benefits are valuable. In doing so, we can teach students to use an index and the online catalog, but more importantly, we can provide them opportunities to take increased responsibility for their education, improve skills in interacting with others, develop critical thinking, and, as Bruffee says, learn to talk to each other, because "we think in ways we have learned to talk" (670). More than any other department on campus, we have our hands in a variety of disciplines, and provide access to a good deal of this conversation of humankind. In bibliographic instruction, our conversation should include theories and methodologies for creating partnerships through collaborative learning.

BIBLIOGRAPHY

Bruffee, Kenneth. "Collaborative Learning and the 'Conversation of Mankind.'" College English 46 (1984): 635-652. "Social Construction, Language, and the Authority of Knowledge: A Bibliographic Essay." College English 48 (1986): 773-790.

DeCristoforo, Alice. Collaborative Learning. Message to: Michele Hanson. In: BI-Listserv (Bibliographic Instruction Discussion Group), Binghamton, NY. 1993 Dec. 15, 9:42 am.

146 THE UPSIDE OF DOWNSIZING

Dewey, John. "Experience and Education." The Kappa Delta Pi lecture series 10. New York: Macmillan, 1938.

Elbow, Peter. Writing Without Teachers. New York: Oxford, 1973.

Flower, Linda. "Writer-Based Prose: A Cognitive Basis for Problems in Writing." The Writing Teacher's Sourcebook, Gary Tate and Edward P.J. Corbett, eds. New York: Oxford University Press, 1981.

Gere, Anne Ruggles. Writing Groups: History, Theory, and Implications. Carbondale: Southern Illinois University Press, 1987.

Johnson, David W., Roger T. Johnson and Karl A. Smith. 1991. Cooperative Learning: Increasing College Faculty Instructional Productivity. ASHE-ERIC Higher Education Report No.4. Washington, D.C.: The George Washington University, School of Education and Human Development.

MacGregor, Jean. "Collaborative Learning: Shared Inquiry as a Process of Reform." Changing the Face of College Teaching, Marilla D. Sviniki, ed. New Directions for Teaching and Learning 42. San Francisco: Jossey-Bass, 1990.

McMillian-Nelson, Sharyl. Collaborative Learning. Message to: Michele Hanson. In: BI-L Listserv (Bibliographic Instruction Discussion Group), Binghamton, NY. 1993 Dec. 11, 14:55 pm.

Sajdak, Bruce. Collaborative Learning. Message to: Michele Hanson. In: BI-Listserv (Bibliographic Instruction Discussion Group), Binghamton, NY. 1993 Dec. 13, 6:35 am.

Sheridan, Jean. "The Reflective Librarian: Some Observations on Bibliographic Instruction in the Academic Library." The Journal of Academic Librarianship 16 (1990): 22-26.

"Rethinking Andragogy: The Case for Collaborative Learning in Continuing Higher Education." The Journal of Continuing Higher Education 37.2 (1989): 2-6.

Stewart, Donald C. "Collaborative Learning and Composition: Boon or Bane?" Rhetoric Review 7 (1988): 58-83.

Trimbur, John. "Consensus and Difference in Collaborative Learning." College English 51 (1989): 602-616.

Warmkessel, Marjorie Markoff and Frances M. Carothers. "Collaborative Learning and Bibliographic Instruction." The Journal of Academic Librarianship 19 (1993): 4-7.

Wiener, Harvey S. "Collaborative Learning in the Classroom: A Guide to Evaluation." College English 48 (1986): 52-61.

12

Teaching the Use of the Internet in a Traditional Library Instruction Program

Tony Harvell
Copley Library, University of San Diego

BACKGROUND INFORMATION

For the past eight years, Copley Library, serving a student body of 5,000 students and 225 faculty with three professional schools plus the College of Arts and Sciences, has offered a one-credit course: Library Research Methods. The course has been team taught by four reference librarians, rotated among them each semester. The course instructs students in the "use of an academic library's printed resources and computers to find information for many disciplines."[1] The course is taken almost exclusively as an undergraduate requirement for students with an interdisciplinary major in the humanities. About half of the students are usually college freshmen, and the remainder are upper division students. Virtually all college majors are represented, but nearly half of the students are usually business majors, reflecting overall university enrollment trends.

Over the past three years there has been an increasing emphasis on instruction in the use of CD-ROM products, and more recently in end-user database search services such as OCLC First-Search and the National Library of Medicine's Grateful Med service. As part of the overall philosophy of the course, the primary goal is teaching library skills. As part of the critical thinking component, students are assisted in evaluating information sources for objectivity, appropriateness for the assignment at hand, and reliability of the information.

The format of the class includes a series of worksheets on specific tasks: using the OPAC, using CD-ROM indexes, using statistical publications and government information, and more recently, worksheets on end-user online services and resources on the Internet. About two years ago, as the University gopher was developed and as reference librarians became more aware of resources on the Internet, it became apparent that we would need to incorporate this resource into the course.

Historically, the training of users on the mainframe computer had been the purview of the Academic Computing Department. Like other academic units, limited staff and facilities required them to prioritize the instruction they could provide. Software programs such as SPSS and some microcomputer-based operations focused on teaching beginning courses on electronic mail and file transfer protocol. However, their courses were generally restricted to faculty or graduate students. Most of the publicity about their courses appeared in the Academic Computing Newsletter, which was normally sent only to faculty and staff of the University.

Reference interviews and other bibliographic instruction programs revealed that the majority of the undergraduate student body, although using campus computer labs, was unaware of the existence of the campus gopher, much less the kinds of resources that were increasingly available over the Internet.

Consequently, the reference librarians decided to incorporate this information in our bibliographic instruction programs whenever possible. Library Research Methods, needed to be improved so we decided to devote four class sessions entirely to the use of the Internet, with the focus being on resources available on the Internet, rather than activities such as electronic mail and file transfer protocol. This seemed consistent with our overall course philosophy. There has not been a question of territoriality on our campus. The general feeling in both academic computing and the library being that there is room for everybody to teach about the Internet. However, in the library we felt it most appropriate to focus on the Internet as an information resource, and leave the teaching of electronic mail and file transfer protocol to Academic Computing or individual instructors who could probably do a better job of it. We still kept the focus on skills needed to identify and access resources on the Internet.

COURSE CONTENT

The first session was devoted to a discussion of what the Internet actually is. A small section addressed its history and current issues affecting the Internet. Students seemed genuinely interested in this information and all of the media attention on the "information superhighway" made it quite timely. The session helped students conceptualize the Internet and why its very lack of formal organization provided some special problems related to connectivity. Though we did not have a textbook, I found the book Crossing the Internet Threshold by Roy Tennant, John Ober, and Anne G. Lipow[2] to be extremely helpful. A bibliography of library materials on the Internet was distributed to the class. The Tennant books, with its succinct and clear explanations of the background and process of the Internet helped me to transmit this information in a meaningful way to the class. The first two sessions were conducted in the classroom with the instructor using an LCD to demonstrate access to the Internet. The third and fourth sessions took place in the Academic Computing Lab where all students could access the Internet simultaneously while the instructor's screen was projected via LCD.

The campus wide information system (gopher) proved to be the major vehicle for teaching the skills needed to access the Internet for the broadest group of users. Rather than having to teach separately about the telnet function, the effective use of the gopher seemed a better alternative. Students seemed to easily grasp the concept of a gopher and found the mechanics of moving through the menus easy. The arrangement and structure of the gopher was presented. Concurrently with the development of this unit of the course, a subcommittee of the Library Automation Committee (Reference Services) was given the charge to develop the "Libraries" portion of the campus-wide gopher. Despite many campus libraries developing their own gophers, we were given the authority to design the Libraries part of the University gopher and forward our recommendations to Academic Computing for the rest of the gopher menus. Feedback from students in the class was essential in deciding how we were to construct our menus. Our general feeling was that simplicity was a virtue. The system would be of little help if users were lost in layers of menus. It would also be helpful to focus on training our users to locate other gophers and use the resources on them. We developed a list of about ten gophers we felt were particularly user friendly or particularly comprehensive—UC-Santa Cruz, University of Michigan Libraries, the Washington and Lee University were among them.

The second session focused on using services such as Veronica and Jughead to locate resources on other gophers. We had a Veronica and Jughead (high level gopher menus) pointer on the third level of our gopher. We concentrated on how to formulate Veronica searches. Once a site was identified and the connection was made, we looked at the the service and how to use it effectively. One example we frequently used was ERIC, since the students had been exposed to the database in the CD-ROM format. We emphasized the difference between bibliographic and textual or statistical files on the Internet. Particular attention was called to electronic journals, what they are and how to find them. In general, the focus was on accessing skills and on file content.

The third sessions were "hands-on." The instructor would present a question and the students would attempt to answer it using what they had been shown. The first questions focused on using gopher bibliographic databases to identify materials held in nearby libraries (e.g. MELVYL, and the University of

California-San Diego and San Diego State University Libraries). The questions then progressed to more specific kinds of questions—statistical questions from the CIA World Factbook, quotations from Shakespeare and the Bible, economic data from the Economic Bulletin Board.

The fourth sessions were supervised lab exercises. The instructor compiled a list of questions from the Internet Hunts, particularly those designed for beginners. The students were instructed to find the questions on the Internet using the USD gopher or any other gopher. It was recommended that they all start with different questions and use different gophers.

We would share our results with each other. At least one question involved using a foreign gopher (in one case a gopher in Australia). Some of the questions were "fun" questions, others quite serious. They had an hour to answer any of ten questions and we compared our experiences. The instructor wandered through the lab answering questions and troubleshooting problems. The last component of the assignment was individually geared to students' majors. Humanities majors received one set of questions, science majors another, and social science and business majors yet another. The questions were a little more difficult than the previous ones. Student were given "extra credit" for answering them. These were to be done independently and individually in the computer labs. In order to verify that the answers came from the Internet and not a printed source, students were required to use the "equals (=)" key while on the gopher, which will identify the path (as well as the host site) and record that information. The goal of this assignment was to make them aware of specific Internet Resources in their disciplines. The University of Michigan subject guides to the Internet helped construct questions.

CONSIDERATIONS

Course evaluations showed that this instruction was considered a success both by the students and instructor. However there were some considerations that need to be looked at.

Students all had different levels of comfort with using computers, in particular interacting with a mainframe. Slow response times on certain activities, "dead end pointers," and error messages provided varying degrees of frustration. In fact, we found that our campus broadband network (which is not yet fibre optic cable) had trouble handling twenty-five people simultaneously accessing the gopher, in particular if they were trying to access the same file. Busy messages from other host computers also proved frustrating. This points out the overall issues related to connectivity of the Internet, and the communications infrastructure problems that may loom on the horizon. Clearly it pointed out our own institution's need to upgrade its infrastructure if the gopher or indeed the Internet is to be used in a large scale way on campus for instructional purposes.

Since the theme of this conference is on the upside of downsizing, I might make a few observations on this point. Being a small Catholic institution almost entirely dependent on tuition, we were not faced so much with downsizing as with the inability to "upsize." Though we have had frequent requests for networking many of our CD-ROMs, the funds to do so were not there. In the case of databases such as ERIC, we were able to make them available to a larger number of users than our single stand-alone station could handle. We were also able to make services such as CARL UnCover and OCLC FirstSearch available to a larger group of users and outside the library walls. In fact, via Internet this information would be available outside the library and relatively conveniently as opposed to the standard printed sources. Many resources are indeed unique to the Internet. For students with a computer account and a home computer, these things were available to them in their homes. It has helped us, in a small way, to address the unmet needs we have of students with very tight personal schedules who have trouble coming to the library at certain times only to use specific and often busy CD-ROM databases or common reference sources that may be up on the Internet.

We were also faced with rather conservative university policies on giving out mainframe accounts. Though they can be issued to undergraduates for specific course-related instruction, normally they were not issued to undergraduates on any type of an ongoing basis. Initially, our University computers allowed dialing in to the host machine and going to our gopher without an active account on the machine. However, due to some security problems, that access was eliminated. Consequently students only had access through terminals on the network either in the library or computer labs. The demand for library users' access to the gopher increased, though our ability to add additional terminals did not.

In our Library Research Methods class, we are introducing the gopher and Internet resources, in general, in nearly all course-related bibliographic instruction, whenever appropriate. In particular graduate students in education have found ERIC very useful. We are working with the faculty to help them identify Internet resources they may find useful in their teaching and research. Two half day "hands-on" workshops with a third scheduled (just for the business faculty) have proven very useful. The faculty had been asking for periodical table of contents searching for some time, and we were unable to subscribe to the commercial services. Therefore when CARL UnCover began providing open access, this helped meet that need. We now include CARL UnCover searching in most bibliographic instruction programs. Our users have greater expectations about what the Internet, the library, and librarians can do. The lack of network access to many of our CD-ROM databases is being addressed through access to First-Search Databases, and we sell or provide free search cards to any of our users who want to search those databases from their own computers in lieu of coming to the library. We have provided a third level gopher menu to connect to these services. Though this is not the long term solution we would seek, we believe it is a step in the right direction.

The Internet is a wonderful resource with great potential in academic libraries. Because of the very nature of its lack of a central governance it provides special problems in access. The development of services such as gopher, Veronica, and Archie have greatly enhanced access to its resources. However this multiplicity of services requires more user education. The library as a primary information provider is a logical, if not exclusive place, to begin this user education. The assimilation of Internet resources into library bibliographic instruction programs can provide a strategic forum for educating today's and tomorrow's users of the Internet.

ENDNOTES

1. Course description in the Undergraduate Bulletin of the University of San Diego, 1994-1996. San Diego: University of San Diego, 1994. p. 74.

2. Roy Tennant, John Ober, and Anne G. Lipow. Crossing the Internet Threshold. San Carlos, CA: Library Solutions Press, 1993.

13

Information Literacy: For the Privileged Only?

Lana W. Jackman and Patricia Payne
University of Massachusetts Boston

> The mark of a good student of the future will be the ability to locate and manage information, skills in analytical and critical thinking, and an ability to cope with ambiguity.
>
> —Joan Eindor, Online Educator, April 1987, p. 5.

The University of Massachusetts Boston, one of five campuses of the University of Massachusetts system, is a comprehensive, doctoral-granting campus with a mission to respond to the academic and economic needs of the state's urban areas and their diverse population.

Our curricula, the way we teach, and our financial and academic support services address the needs both of traditional and non-traditional students. They come to the University from varied social, cultural, and ethnic backgrounds, and characteristically combine University education with work and family responsibilities.[1]

The library is essential to achievement of the goals of urban public higher education at UMB. In supporting the University mission to the Commonwealth, the library also provides services to the citizenry and serves as a statewide informational resource.

The Healey Library has seen a deterioration in funding since 1983. Positions have been lost or frozen. The materials budget has shrunk. Some years the only funds available were from the greatly reduced State Special; a yearly line item appropriation specifically for academic libraries in state supported institutions.

We agree that the staff members are the library's key resource. Unfortunately, the Healey Library has lost nearly twenty-five percent of its positions since 1983. In spite of these limitations the library does attempt to offer a diversity of approaches for providing access to information, via a self-guided tour publication, handbooks for faculty and students, and specialized handouts.

Due to staff limitations, the orientation and training of library users is reassessed and restructured on a continuing basis. At times traditional bibliographic instruction has been eliminated.

There is an assumption that the new diversely prepared students entering the portals of higher education possess adequate research skills to cruise successfully the rapids of intellectual inquiry. Demographically these students run the gamut from eager eighteen year olds to apprehensive, often timid, senior citizens. Many are new immigrants and have minimal confidence in their English language ability. A significant number of these prospective degree-seekers are first generation college students. The institution may actively recruit these diversely prepared students and channel them through developmental studies types of programs, yet the ultimate retention rate for these students has been abysmal. For this group of students, many without strong academic preparatory backgrounds, the instruction of basic skills is a critical issue. The incorporation of any type of basic skill instruction, an unwanted stepchild in the pedagogical process within the Academy, is essential to the success of these students.

The traditional concept of basic skills and its application indirectly assaults the intellectual capacity of the diversely prepared student. We need to look at the basic skills issue with a more holistic vision. Taylor and Sherman define basic skills as those communication and learning skills that an individual needs to carry out specific academic, career, or broader life tasks.[2] Library literacy demands that the knowledge of certain skills is a pre-requisite to becoming a successful student adept in the ways of information literacy. Defined as the ability to find, evaluate, and use effectively, information for one's own personal enrichment as well as that of society's information literacy should be the major outcome of a formal education. We believe that this can be achieved through developing a strong, working bond between the institutions' Freshman Year Programs and the academic library.

Many studies have validated the positive impact that the freshman year experience has had on student retention. The three programs we describe here represent different models of collaboration among University administration, faculty, professional staff, and librarians to integrate information literacy into the freshman year experience.

COLLEGE OF PUBLIC AND COMMUNITY SERVICE

As an integral part of a competency-based program, the faculty and librarian of the College of Public and Community Service designed a series of experiences that students in this college might gain through formal course work or through independent study. The advantage of this program is its flexibility in accommodating differing learning styles. Faculty, in cooperation with the library liaison, may coordinate the activities in the library research competency with their own class assignments. (See Appendix I)

ACADEMIC ADVISOR/ LIBRARIAN COLLABORATION

In response to a request for proposals to improve retention activities for students, research or faculty development, we submitted a pilot project to integrate BI into the new students' academic experience. We strongly believe that in an era of international competition and explosive changes in the information environment, university students, in particular, urban students from diverse cultural backgrounds, must develop information literacy skills not only for themselves as survival strategies but also as a retention effort.

With a University grant of $3,500, we developed a two-semester library literacy pilot project. Our goals were: (a) to provide students with a basic understanding of library organization, technology, and resources; and (b) to enable students to demonstrate basic research skills through the process of developing search strategies, compiling annotated bibliographies, and developing a critical thinking research paper.

The participants were seventeen urban public high school non-traditional scholarship students selected from two University-sponsored scholarship programs. The Taylor Scholarship program is funded through the Boston Globe Foundation. The Carson Scholarship Program is funded by a variety of sources within the University. These two scholarship programs are unique in that they both encourage the selection of urban students who demonstrate academic promise. An independent study format was used, with three faculty members recruited to act as mentors to meet periodically with their assigned students. Two upper-classmen served as tutors for students experiencing writing and research difficulties. The first semester was devoted to integrating those skills in the development of the students' research papers.

Even with this extraordinary level of support, the students experienced a great deal of difficulty. They were typical of urban students being accepted into the University, and many of them had participated in a developmental studies pre-college program. It was clear that the basic literacy skills needed where non-existent at the beginning and barely visible at the completion of the project.

A significant strength of the project was the cooperation of faculty, library staff, and the University Advising Center. Failure to incorporate a substantive bibliographic instructional component into an academic skills program is pedagogically damaging to the under-prepared student. A basic how-to introduction to the library and its resources does not prepare the student to become an academic researcher. Furthermore, it does not allow for the effective development and integration of critical/analytical skills necessary for successful, consistent progression through an academic discipline.

INTRODUCTION TO UNIVERSITY STUDIES

In 1990, the University of Massachusetts Boston developed a University Advising Center to focus on increasing the retention rate of its diversified student population. Part of the Center's responsibility was the Introduction to University Studies course, a one-semester orientation course valued at one academic credit. Enrollment was limited to new freshmen. Since 1990, each semester has brought a new approach, a new challenge to making library literacy an integral component of a new student's academic experience. This semester's approach was based on a model provided by Fred Wild, Assistant Professor of Communications and Janet Hurlbert, Assistant Professor/Instructional Services at Lycoming College in Pennsylvania. (See Appendix II)

We learned a great deal from the pilot project. It was much too labor-intensive to be practical and applicable campus-wide. It did, however, support our thesis that there is the potential for increased cooperation among many segments of the campus to experiment with creative ideas. As the other two programs continue to flourish and expand, we believe they hold great promise in this era of downsizing. As we approach the twenty-first century and the increasing demands for library and information services, information literacy skills will be of paramount importance. The following recommendations represent survival strategies for academic libraries today and tomorrow.

- Academic libraries need to build cooperative instruction relationships with non-academic units on campus.
- Academic librarians need to become more involved in programmatic design targeting pre-college and freshman year programs.

- Actively recruit faculty, professional staff and library support staff to develop course-integrated and course-related instructional programming.
- Train upperclassmen and graduate students to act as mentors for new students, using the library's resources and services.
- Design instructional programs for graduate and undergraduate students, utilizing new technologies and distance learning techniques.
- Target non-traditional resources such as grant development, community linkages to support information literacy activities.
- Build bridge relationships between the elementary and secondary segments of the community offering access to services and talents of the library staff.

In conclusion, the new student of the 1990's and beyond is the urban/minority student who will be faced with the dynamics of the multicultural, social/environmental challenges now occurring in major urban centers today. Public education is on overload adjusting to the new immigrants as well as dealing with the continuing problems of limited resources and the increased need for support services. Students are being recruited by institutions with little or no regard for their proficiency in library research methodology—a skill critical to the life of "also successful" college student.

"Information Literacy . . . for the privileged only?" means that if we continue to submit to the fiscal constraints placed on us by the mismanagement of institutional and/or governmental resources and stifle our own individual creativity, proactivity and insight, then we as educational professionals, will only have ourselves to blame for the growing fission in society related access to information and the fair distribution of its resources and benefits.

ENDNOTES

1. University of Massachusetts Boston Mission Statement. 2/26/93
2. Sherman, D. and Taylor, C. "Basic Skills for the Diversity Prepared." In Diverse Student Preparation: Benefits and Issues. San Francisco: Jossey-Bass. 1982.

APPENDIX I

Reading II: LIBRARY RESEARCH:
Rationale: There are many kinds of research and many ways to locate the data needed for professional and academic work. The focus for this competency is on the standard tools and strategies of library research and reading which are essential and, in some instances, prerequisite to the use of other research techniques. Such methods as the interview, the questionnaire, and computer and media resources are required in other CPCS competencies.

Competency:
Using selected library research materials, can locate and read those materials for research purposes.

Criteria:
A. Locating library research materials.
   1. Given a specific research topic, the reader must be able to use a library classification system and indicate how to find resources in the library.
   2. The reader must be able to interpret directions and basic functions of an on-line catalog in order to locate library resources relevant to a single research topic.
   3. The reader must be able to use indexing and abstracting services in order to find information about a research topic.
   4. The reader must be able to suggest appropriate uses for reference sources given a specific research topic.
B. Reading research articles.
   1. The reader must identify the overall purpose and usefulness of research materials.
   2. The reader must be able to summarize the main ideas and supporting evidence from readings of research materials relevant to a specific research topic.
   3. The reader must identify point of view and/or bias in research materials on a given topic.

Standards:
A. Locating library research materials.
   1. The library classification system must be the Library of Congress.
   2. Library resources must include a minimum of 2 of the following: books, law materials, government documents both federal and state, annual reports, etc.

3. At least 3 current citations in 3 different indexing or abstracting services appropriate to a topic must be made. Indexing and
   abstracting services include but are not limited to Reader's
   Guide, Business Periodical Index, newspaper indexes, Social
   Sciences Index, and ERIC. These searches must be done both
   manually and on-line.
4. At least 3 reference sources must be chosen appropriate to a
   research topic (e.g. encyclopedias, biographical dictionaries,
   handbooks, etc.) In order to determine usefulness, the student
   must consider such things as expertise of the author, publication date etc.

B. Reading research articles
   1. For criteria 1, 2, and 3 at least 3 research materials must be used.

Methods of evaluation:
1. Student takes the ALM course Research Report Writing and
   completes course activities.
2. Student submits a research portfolio. Student should contact the
   ALM Center office for a specific description of the contents of the
   portfolio.
3. Student obtains evaluation packet from the ALM Center and ar-
   ranges for an evaluation using UMass/Boston's Healey Library.

APPENDIX II

THE DECADE ASSIGNMENT:
The remainder of this course will be dedicated to participatory learning activities designed to introduce you to the various informational
resources available to you in the Healey Library. Thematically, we
will focus our energies on the decade of the 40's. We will take "hot
issues" of the 90's and research how they were handled during the
40's. We will concentrate on using the following basic informational
resources available in any standard academic library:

  : OPAC - Group I
  : Periodical Index - Group II
  : Newspaper Abstracts and Microfilm - Group III

The class will be divided into 3 groups. Each group will be responsible for providing the total class with a written/typed list of advan-
tages/disadvantages on using one of the above listed resources as well

as leading the class discussion on their topic. The group will also be required to submit an annotated bibliography of, at least, 10 references at the end of the project.

For example:

Group I will be focusing on OPAC

They will present to the class a written list of advantages/disadvantages of using.

They will lead the class discussion on the topic of OPAC.

They will present a bibliography of 10 references on the chosen "theme" that they have researched.

They will also provide the class with a written search strategy.

The last two sessions of this course will be devoted to an overall discussion of the findings of the groups on the differences/similarities of the 40's and the 90's.

14

Bringing in the Reserves: Generating Confident and Skillful New Instructors

Trudi E. Jacobson and David A. Tyckoson
University Library
University at Albany, SUNY

Downsizing. Budget reductions. Re-engineering. Right-sizing. In the last few years, virtually every academic library in the nation has been faced with one of these "new challenges." Colleges and universities of all sizes are having a much more difficult time in meeting all of the economic demands placed upon them. Higher personnel costs, increasing equipment costs, new computing requirements, and higher administrative costs are combined with enrollment reductions, reduced state aid, larger class sizes, and an increasing need for remedial instruction to create a situation in which academic departments must fight with each other for ever-scarcer resources.

Libraries are certainly not exempt from this situation. With their large numbers of employees, extended hours of service, and acquisitions budgets that frequently run in the millions of dollars, libraries have become obvious targets in times of fiscal crisis. Journal cancellations, hiring freezes, reductions in hours, and the consolidation of service points have been typical library responses to budget problems. It is a rare academic library in the 1990s that has not seen one or more of the above situations.

Unfortunately, budget and staff reductions are rarely accompanied by a reduction in service demands. Our statistics measuring activities such as reference queries, material circulations, photocopy requests, interlibrary loans, and database searches often continue to rise even as the level of funding falls. The instruction librarian is not exempt from this process and is often being asked to teach more classes even as the available staffing to do so disappears.

Instruction librarians are also faced with several new service demands. In addition to the continuing need for instruction in research methods and subject-related resources, new technologies have created a whole new demand for instruction. Users of online catalogs, end-user searching, CD-ROMs, the Internet, Gopher, Mosaic, and a variety of other new services require instruction to users with an ever wider range of knowledge levels, from the beginner who is unfamiliar with the keyboard to the sophisticated searcher who desires to learn complex search strategies and techniques. This increased demand can be more than existing instruction librarians can handle.

Libraries that are experiencing downsizing are rarely in the position to hire completely new instruction staff to meet these new and increased demands. To deal with this problem, instruction librarians must either recruit staff from other departments in the library and teach them the skills necessary to participate in instruction or let the demands go unfilled. At the University at Albany, we designed a program to train staff members from other departments in teaching methods and instructional skills. These staff members included newly hired reference librarians, collection development librarians who had previously not participated in user education, and graduate student assistants and interns assigned to the Reference Department. While all of these staff members were expected to participate in instruction, none had been hired specifically for this activity. With the exception of the graduate students, each of the staff members was adding instructional responsibility on top of their other duties.

The primary goal of the program was to improve the teaching skills of the staff members involved in the program. Most librarians receive little or no instruction in teaching methods and/or learning styles, yet they are all expected to be able to instruct users in complex information tools and strategies. Librarians without a background in teaching techniques usually respond to the situation in the only manner in which they can conceive. The result, a tour of the reference area and the discussion or display of as many reference books as possible during the hour. Traditional library instruction, in which the librarian lectures to the class about the contents of each book, index, or database, are effective only for their lists of sources. Without some sort of hands-on activity, even the most motivated of students loses interest.

A librarian, to become truly effective, needs to employ active learning methods and to encourage their students to think critically. The use of hands-on activities that challenge students to find and evaluate information leaves a much more long-lasting impression than the best of lectures. Instruction in which the students participate in sample research processes or in which they discover for themselves the value of various resources leaves a much more lasting impression than the simple lecture. This instruction will enable students to begin to incorporate this information into their existing knowledge base and to help them overcome anxieties. However, these are not features that most librarians have encountered in their own education. This program was designed to provide each student with experience in observing and using active learning techniques in library instruction.

The Head of the Reference Department and the Coordinator of the User Education Program met this challenge by initiating a series of weekly two hour meetings. These meetings ran over the course of one semester. New public service librarians, reference department interns, and graduate assistants were asked to attend these meetings, while existing (or more experienced) librarians were invited to attend. A schedule of topics was distributed so that librarians were able to select just those sessions covering topics which most interested them.

Librarians from a neighboring institution were also invited to attend.

The topics covered during the sessions included:

Philosophy of User Education and Reference Services Visions
    for the Future
How to Prepare an Instruction Session
Basic Teaching Techniques Active Learning (Parts I and II)
Reference/Patron Interaction
Dealing with Difficult Reference Situations
Participant-led Instruction (4 sessions)

While either the Coordinator of User Education Programs
or the Head of Reference normally ran each session, we encouraged and expected full participation from everyone. We
practiced what we preached about teaching, and used a variety of active learning techniques: discussions drawing on participant experiences and observations; small group work where
the participants were given an instructional scenario and asked
to develop a solution or lesson plan; pair work wherein participants developed and presented brief sessions; free-writing
exercises; and full-fledged instructional sessions taught by each
participant. These last classes, which ran over four weeks, were
exciting. Each librarian and student had to develop and present
a half hour class on the topic of his or her choice. Everyone
was extremely nervous about her/his instructional unit. They
knew the other class participants would be informally judging
their presentations, and that this might be a tougher audience
than one composed of students. The two of us who had in-
itiated the program wanted to see how much had been learned
during the sessions, and how well it would be applied. In order to be fair to the students, as class leaders, we also put ourselves on display and tried out some new ideas for teaching
specific topics. Both of us experienced the same nervousness
and received the same critiques as other participants, allowing
us to learn about our own styles and techniques.

The results of the program can best be judged by the presentations of the students. The quality of the sessions varied among
the participants, with some adapting more easily to active learning than others. Each one incorporated at least some of the techniques that we were emphasizing, yet each put his or her own
twist on the situation. The students learned not only from the

instructors, but also from each other. Much of the discussion centered on ideas and alternatives that each of us may have incorporated. A session on the use of SIC Codes in business research given by one of the graduate students will long be remembered by all who attended as a tour de force in presenting complex information in an engaging and instructive manner. The staff who participated in this program have also been much more likely to cooperate on real-life instruction sessions. This program built a strong team spirit among participants that will carry over long after the workshops have ended.

As instructors, this program was also highly valuable. We were able to directly watch our colleagues learn and adapt to new concepts and ideas. It also provided both of us with a means for evaluating and providing feedback to other staff members in a controlled environment. While the program took a considerable amount of time in planning and execution, it was also one of the most fun uses of our time and was eagerly anticipated each week by both students and instructors alike!

During the spring 1994 semester, a similar program is underway that is designed to teach subject reference skills. In this series of workshops, subject specialists are presenting sources and strategies for answering reference queries in their fields. Some of the topics being covered include law, business, census data, literary criticism, and historical research. Several of the librarians who participated as students in the first program are serving as teachers in this series. This will give them a chance to practice their skills as well as giving us another opportunity to observe their teaching techniques. This series will also bring in some long-term librarians who did not participate in the first program and will enable them to observe as well as to teach. We hope that everyone will learn something (either subject material or teaching methods) from this series.

Using staff from other departments is one way in which to expand instructional services without hiring new personnel. However, that staff cannot be expected to be well-versed in teaching methods and techniques. Programs such as this should help new recruits build confidence, understand the learning process, and avoid failure in teaching. We recommend that other instruction managers implement similar programs to teach new teachers.

15

Teaching, Learning, and Technostress

John Kupersmith
The General Libraries, The University of Texas at Austin

Stress is inevitable as libraries and their users deal with the challenges of diminishing human resources, exploding information resources, and accelerating technological change. The phenomenon of computer-related stress or "technostress" has attracted considerable attention among librarians in recent years. This paper suggests that teaching about electronic information systems may be a good way for librarians to gain mastery and overcome technostress. It describes the experiences of library staff participating in an intensive teaching program at The University of Texas at Austin, and discusses how an instructional program can be designed and managed to maximize staff development.

WHAT IS TECHNOSTRESS?

Craig Brod originally defined this term as "... a modern disease of adaptation caused by an inability to cope with the new computer technologies in a healthy manner."[1] While certain personality types may be more vulnerable than others,[2] some level of technostress has become common in reference staff with the rapid proliferation of new (and not always well-designed) information systems, the escalation of user demands, and the frequent need to function as a technical expert in areas where one feels uncertain at best.

Different individuals react to stress in different ways. Stress can energize a person, focus attention, and stimulate behaviors of engagement and adaptation. When the reaction is less healthy, stress can drain energy and lead to apathy and avoidance. Typical symptoms of an unhealthy reaction to technostress include feelings of isolation and frustration, negative attitudes toward new computer-based sources and systems, self-deprecating thoughts or statements about one's ability to cope, a definition of self as not involved with computers, indifference to users' computer-related needs, and an apologetic attitude toward users.[3]

IS TEACHING A CURE?

Just as learning changes the student, teaching changes the teacher. The teaching process—defining objectives, selecting methods, preparing and delivering instruction—demands constructive behaviors, calls forth positive attitudes, and naturally leads the teacher to master the material taught.

This is not to say that every teaching situation is ideal, or that "natural" necessarily means "easy." Most people feel some stress if they are asked to teach technical material with which they are not highly familiar. The stimulus of preparing instruction does not by itself render the content easier to master. Knowing the material in a technical sense does not necessarily eliminate all stress or produce perfect self-confidence.

However, the experience of library staff at The University of Texas at Austin suggests that aggressive involvement in such teaching can reduce the effects of stress and increase self-confidence as well as technical skills.

AN INTENSIVE TEACHING PROGRAM

Like many other academic libraries, The General Libraries at UT Austin has offered library instruction for several years, and has incorporated new information tools, such as online databases, the online catalog, CD-ROMs, and the Internet, into its user education activities. In September 1992, the Reference and Information Services Department of the Perry-Casteneda Library (the university's main library) began an ambitious program of "Electronic Information Demos" designed to accomplish two different but complementary objectives: to reach as many users as possible with at least a basic orientation to the new technology, and to accelerate the staff's acquisition of skills with the new systems. In the five semesters since, the program has grown to involve a volunteer staff of 45 (both professional and classified) from several library departments, teaching as many as 160 sessions per semester and reaching a cumulative total of over 8,000 students, faculty, researchers, and members of the community. Topics covered include Internet resources (telnet, ftp, gopher, WAIS, etc.), Internet connectivity and techniques (SLIP, file decompression, etc.), LEXIS/NEXIS, CD-ROMs, and the UTCAT PLUS online catalog/database system.

Dennis Dillon, Assistant Head of the Reference and Information Services Department and the initiator of the demo series, describes it in these terms:

> The main elements of the current program have been the same for a year and a half now: frequent short courses open to everyone; a modular schedule so that the same course is repeated at intervals and given at different times; a mix of instructors so that the same person does not teach the same course all the time and become stale; a constant experimentation with course offerings and in what a particular course covers; a multitude of handouts some of which are basic to the program, some of which are prepared anew for each particular session; a course climate of give and take with frequent audience questions; and a willingness to learn from the audience which often includes people with years of sophisticated computer and subject experience.[4]

SURVEY OF INSTRUCTORS

How does participation in this innovative and intensive program affect those doing the teaching? This paper reports the results of an informal survey of "Electronic Information Demo" instructors at UT Austin in December 1993. The word informal is used deliberately: this is not a report of scientific research, and no claims are made for statistical validity. The sample size is small (n = 19), participants generally knew of the author's views regarding technostress, and their self-reported stress levels were not measured scientifically. Despite this parade of qualifications, the survey results show interesting patterns and indicate that the teaching process had beneficial effects for these individuals.

Respondents were asked to rate three elements on a scale of 1 (low) to 5 (high): their "level of stress, related to using (and helping others use) electronic information systems"; their "level of skill in using electronic information systems," and their "level of self-confidence in using electronic information systems." They were asked to provide ratings on each element for the time before they became demo instructors, and after teaching the demos.

When the survey results were tallied, the 19 instructors who responded fell naturally into two groups: 10 individuals who had taught between 1 and 6 demo sessions (averaging 3.7) in Fall 1992, and 9 individuals who had taught between 11 and 29 sessions (averaging 17.9) during the same period. Both groups consisted mostly of professional librarians. Figure 15-1 shows the results of the survey for each group.

The first group—those who had taught relatively few sessions—reported moderate benefits. On the scale of 5 points, their average level of stress declined from 2 before becoming involved in the program, to 1.5. Those with a heavier teaching load reported greater benefits, starting at a higher stress level than their counterparts and experiencing more than twice the reduction in stress (from 3.1 to 1.9) Likewise, while the occasional teachers reported skill levels averaging 2.9 before the demos and 3.5 afterwards, the frequent teachers reported twice the benefit, with their average skill level changing from 2.8 to 4.

Fig. 15-1. Stress, skill, and self-confidence of instructors

Scale: 1 = low
    3 = moderate
    5 = high

	OCCASIONAL TEACHERS AVG. 3.7d n = 10	FREQUENT TEACHERS AVG. 17.9d n = 9
Level of stress, related to using (and helping others use) electronic information systems:		
BEFORE you became a demo instructor	2	3.1
WHILE preparing & teaching these demos	2.5	2.7
AFTER teaching these demos	1.5	1.9
Net change	-.5	-1.2
Level of skill in using electronic information systems:		
BEFORE you became a demo instructor	2.9	2.8
AFTER teaching these demos		
Net Change	+.6	+1.2
Level of self confidence in using electronic information systems:		
BEFORE you became a demo instructor	2.9	2.9
WHILE preparing & teaching these demos	3.3	2.9
AFTER teaching these demos	3.8	4.1
Net change	+.9	+1.2

Both groups reported the same initial level of self-confidence before the demos; the occasional teachers went from 2.9 to 3.8; the frequent teachers, from 2.9 to 4.1.

The instructors were also asked for written comments on the teaching experience and its effects on them. Here are some of their remarks:

Helped me get to know other instructors, learn and manipulate computer equipment and palette, get to know more students, discover my own areas to improve my knowledge and expertise, learned new ways of expressing Internet concepts, discovered new finds and much more!

Before you can explain how to use a system, you have to know the system. I've learned a lot through experimentation and searching for specific bits of information to demonstrate the capabilities of the system.

It's encouraged me to be more flexible in terms of the total number of tasks that I can expect to complete from day to day. Some days may be centered around scheduling, preparing, and presenting a demo; others may be devoted to some of my other duties. I've learned not to try to do everything each day.

I . . . learned as much as I taught.

You never learn anything quite so well as when you teach it.

It is possible, of course, that this was an atypical group of people. However, a similar survey of students in an Internet course in The University of Texas at Austin Graduate School of Library and Information Science also showed benefits from participating in a single Internet demo prepared and performed as a class assignment.[5] These students (n = 18) averaged a stress level of 2.5 before their demos, 1.9 afterwards; a skill level of 3 before, 3.8 afterwards; and a self-confidence level of 3.2 before, 3.9 afterwards.

It is also possible that those who undertake a heavy teaching load possess some personal characteristics that may help them gain more significantly from the teaching experience than those who teach less. The survey results indicate, however, that both the occasional and frequent teachers realized some benefits.

MANAGING FOR STAFF DEVELOPMENT

As suggested above, not every teaching situation is ideal. We do not always have the opportunity to design and administer a ''high-tech'' instructional program for maximum benefits to

FIGURE 15-2 SUMMARIZES THEIR RESPONSES

Fig. 15-2. How elements of program affected stress

Scale: −3 = decreased your stress level
     0 = neutral
    +3 = increased your stress level

	OCCASIONAL TEACHERS Avg. 3.7 demos n=0	FREQUENCY TEACHERS Avg. 17.9 demos n=9
Equipment provided (computers, software, palette)	-0.4	-0.9
Scheduling system for rooms & equipment	-0.2	-0.9
Handouts provided	-1.6	-1.7
Teaching in pairs or teams	-2.3	-1.4
Meetings held to discuss demo plans	-0.7	-1.1
E-mail distribution list for instructors	-0.6	-1.1
Having a specific person named as demo coordinator	-1.5	-0.1

teachers as well as learners. However, when this is possible, what elements are most important in reducing the stress factor and helping teachers do their job? As a way of approaching this question, the instructors in the General Libraries demo program were also asked to rate several elements of the program on a scale of -3 ("decreased your stress level") to +3 ("increased your stress level"), with a value of 0 being neutral.

These responses indicate that the most beneficial support features were the handouts (many of which were prepared by individual instructors, then "adopted" and made available to all, with multiple copies on file in the demo room) and the practice of teaching in pairs or teams. As Dennis Dillon describes it, the latter feature promotes the quality of instruction and provides a framework for instructors to learn from one another.

All of our sessions are taught by two instructors. We always pair an instructor who is experienced in a particular subject, with another instructor who wishes to improve his or her experience and skills. In this way, every session we give for the public is simultaneously a training session for a new instructor. New instructors are paired with many different experienced instructors so that they can both broaden their learning experience, and observe first hand different teaching styles. In this way our instructor base is continually expanding and is continually being infused with new ideas and approaches.[6]

Two channels used for communication with the instructors—meetings held at least once each semester, and an electronic mail distribution list for current news and sharing of experiences—were also rated as being supportive, especially by those who taught more frequently. Interestingly, those who taught less often were more appreciative of the fact that a specific person was designated as coordinator of the program.

CULTURE AND VALUES

It should be evident to anyone who has read this far that the UT Austin demo program encourages a certain esprit de corps among its instructors. A distinct "organizational culture" is one of the greatest factors in the program's success, in both instructional and staff-development terms. From the point of view of both a participant and observer of the program, this culture appears to be based on five key values:

1. Realism about objectives—
Instructors are encouraged not to overload the audience (or themselves). The basic demonstrations focus more on "what is possible" than on "how to"; they do not attempt to turn the audience into instant Internet experts, but rather to impart some useful knowledge and stimulate further learning. Access issues ("How do I connect?") are dealt with in summary form, with more detailed consultations after class. In response to the

need for more advanced instruction, hands-on sessions, taught in a specially equipped facility, now constitute almost one third of the program.

2. Self-confidence—

From initial recruitment onward, whatever their technological starting-point, instructors are encouraged to develop their skills and self-confidence. Considerable energy is spent in nurturing a positive attitude. As Dillon puts it, "If the instructor is OK, the session will be OK."

3. Instructor as learner—

The instructor is not expected to pose as an omniscient expert, but rather to serve as a guide and facilitator, learning with the audience, and sometimes from the audience. This attitude reduces the performance anxiety usually associated with teaching technical material. Instructors who do not take themselves too seriously are free to admit mistakes, incorporate network "glitches" into the instruction, and spontaneously venture into new territory.

4. Teamwork—

As noted above, team teaching is the norm in this program. It helps build the skills of new volunteers, provides valuable redundancy in dealing with technical questions, and subtly but effectively promotes the spirit of joint learning and exploration.

5. Flexibility—

The program consciously fosters the ability to adapt to new sources and topics, to deal with the vagaries of electronic access, and to respond to unpredictable user needs and questions. Each semester, due to users' requests and instructors' interest, 10 or more new topics are added while others are merged or dropped. Those teaching the demos have become adept at dealing with surprises; as Dillon describes it,

> Our instructors no longer get fazed when connections don't work or machines refuse to cooperate—they just start talking and keep it up until the session is over. . . . Even if all the electricity fails

and the people who turn up for the class don't know the difference between DOS and Mac—the session can always be turned into a question and answer tutorial and the attendees will leave with knowledge they did not have before. We've had times where the instructor led 25 people away from a machine disaster, up back stairwells and down long hallways and into a one person office where they finally found a machine that worked and everyone sat on the floor, on desktops, on bookcases and at the end of the session the attendees were asking when we're going to do this again and telling us that it had been a particularly good session. At other times the instructor has had to keep talking off the top of his/her head while a few feet away in full view of the audience three or four people are using screwdrivers and trying software fixes at the same time in order to get something to work. If there is one rule of thumb we use in Internet instruction it is to stay flexible and be ready for anything.

This flexible attitude goes hand in hand with the "engagement" response to technostress. It is difficult for the kind of rigidity associated with the "avoidance" response to survive in this environment.

CONCLUSION:
BUILDING A "LEARNING ORGANIZATION"

One useful tool for understanding the staff development benefits of the UT Austin program, and the potential of the teaching process in general, is the "learning organization" concept. As described by Peter Senge, a learning organization is one in which staff at all levels are actively involved in the earning process. According to Senge, this kind of organization can adapt to change, and generate productive change, by the practice of "disciplines" that include personal mastery, shared vision, and team learning.[7] In a 1991 interview, Senge used words that can well be applied to the instructors at UT Austin:

> I have come to think that the real generative point in moving toward a learning organization is in small groups that form around commitments. These are groups of people who are really committed to something larger than themselves and larger than

their own personal desires. They support each other in the way that real friends support each other. They tell the truth to each other and they are continually in a mode of enquiry, knowing that nobody knows and everybody can learn continually.[8]

It may be too early to tell what the ultimate effects of this program will be, but its implications for developing staff are clear. Individual librarians wishing to reduce their levels of technostress should consider that teaching the use of electronic resources can produce benefits justifying the time, effort, and stress of the teaching process itself. Instruction coordinators and reference managers should consider that a well-designed and well-run instructional program can benefit the teachers as much as the students.

ENDNOTES

1. Craig Brod, Technostress: The Human Cost of the Computer Revolution. (Reading, MA: Addison-Wesley, 1984), 16.
2. Virginia Moreland, "Technostress and Personality Type," Online 17 (July 1993), 59-62.
3. John Kupersmith, "Technostress and the Reference Librarian," Reference Services Review 20 (Summer 1992), 7-14, 50.
4. This and other descriptive quotes throughout this paper are taken with permission from Dennis Dillon, "Internet Training at Texas," message posted to NETTRAIN listserver, November 9, 1993.
5. Special thanks to the participating students and to Mary Lynn Rice-Lively, the teacher of this course and Library and Information Science Librarian at UT Austin, for their cooperation.
6. Dennis Dillon, private e-mail message, February 24, 1994. Dillon's description of the "Electronic Information Demo" program is likely to appear in print this year.
7. Peter Senge, The Fifth Discipline: The Art and Practice of the Learning Organization. New York: Doubleday/Currency, 1990. For a shorter and perhaps more accessible treatment, see Peter Senge, "The Leader's New Work: Building Learning Organizations," Sloan Management Review 32 (Fall 1990), 7-23. Peter Senge, "The Learning Organization Made Plain," Training & Development (October 1991), 38.

16

Diversity and Diversifying in a Downsized Library

**Christine K. Oka, Patrick J. Dawson,
Lisa Melendez, and Adan Griego**
University of California at Santa Barbara

DIVERSITY AND EDUCATION

The current theme in academic libraries is to maintain or expand existing services with diminishing resources. At the same time, there has been a sudden "discovery" of ethnic diversity in academia. Although the ethnic composition of the population of the United States has been changing for the last half century, only recently has this change been acknowledged, accepted, and embraced. Even marketing and advertising has taken on an ethnic flair as industries "discover" and target various groups.

Colleges and universities have accepted the new diversity and are modifying the traditional curriculum to reflect this change. In 1989, the University of California assembled faculty and librarians to examine Cultural Diversity in Undergraduate Education: What's Working, What Could Work, a two day conference reviewing the traditional curriculum. This was in response to Neil Smelser's report Curricular Diversity in Higher Education sponsored by the Office of the University of California President. In essence, the report noted that as the enrollment in the University has become more diverse, so too instruction should "market directly" and reflect this diversity. In his opening comments, Professor Smelser observed . . .

> students, despite high school experiences with diversity, have not come into sufficient contact with their cultures, and do not understand and appreciate their outlooks and their contributions to the society's history and institutional life. Diversification along these lines is consistent with the 'theory' of pedagogy . . . for the collegiate years.[1]

Students began demanding diversification of the traditional curriculum. Many University of California campuses now require completion of an ethnic studies course for graduation. Often, this was proposed, endorsed, and passed by the student body even when a campus already had courses in African-American, Chicano, American Indian or Asian-American Studies. This practice has spread beyond the collegiate level. Recently, a high school class in Alhambra, California drafted a measure they hoped to introduce into the California legislature, requiring a class on multicultural awareness for high school graduation in California. How can the growing widespread demand for new cultural diversity courses, increased enrollment and expanding library services be met in a time of downsizing? By diversifying within the organization.

DIVERSITY AT THE UCSB LIBRARY

The University of California-Santa Barbara Library has had a long-standing commitment to ethnic diversity in collections and staffing. The Library has worked with the Chicano Studies and Black Studies Departments since the student activism of the 1960s to develop and maintain research level collections in these areas of study. Currently, most ethnic studies collections at the

University of California campuses are housed within their respective departments or program areas; the UCSB Library is the only library within the University of California system with these collections integrated within the library infrastructure (acquisitions, cataloging, circulation, reference services).

Under the leadership of the University Librarian, the University of California-Santa Barbara Library also has supported a Minority Internship program since 1985.[2] As recent library school graduates (1985, 1988, 1990), we all began our professional careers as interns in the UCSB Davidson Library Minority Internship program. The internship included providing reference service for the ethnic studies units: Coleccion Tlahoque Nahuaque (Chicano Studies Library) and the Black Studies Library. As minorities, we were regarded as "experts" in ethnic studies research and even after our assignment in these units was over, we were often sought out (or hunted down!!) by students and the library staff for reference service.

DOWNSIZING AND DIVERSIFYING AT THE UCSB LIBRARY

Our library began experiencing a large number of librarian retirements in 1991 when the first of a series of early-retirements programs was introduced. The reference department lost six librarians and almost 200 years of reference, collection development, and library instruction experience. There were more desk hours and collections to be covered by the remaining librarians. At the same time, the library had just brought up a new OPAC and several new tape-loaded article databases; there were increased demands for library classes. We were facing what Yogi Berra would call "an insurmountable opportunity."

The remaining librarians who took on library instruction were a group with varying levels of teaching experience looking at an overwhelming number of classes. Our approach to meeting this "opportunity" was team-teaching. The article entitled "Learning to Instruct on the Job: Team-Teaching Library Skills,"[3] goes into detail about our efforts to provide a supportive learning environment for the novice instructors while minimizing teaching overload to the more experienced librarians.

For most of these classes, we demonstrated the use of print reference materials in combination with computerized sources. Usually, one team member assembled selected reference materials and handouts and the other prepared the computer demonstration. These preparation tasks were not assigned or set in stone; the team members often swapped responsibilities which helped them build on one another's strengths and weaknesses. Also, they worked more with the faculty to find out what students needed to know about the library in order to complete their class assignment(s). Our roles were diversifying with team-teaching: we were working more interactively with students, their instructors, and with one another. Also, colleagues who had been uneasy about facing a class alone, began expressing interest in easing into teaching via team teaching. As a result, more librarians were recruited into the library instructor pool. An added bonus to team teaching was the public relations aspect: faculty and students started to see librarians as approachable individuals when we interacted with (and sometimes interrupted) each other, rather than a solitary lecturer or ''the answer person'' at the reference desk.

TEAM-TEACHING AND DIVERSITY

What is diversity and how is it taught are two frequently asked questions. Diversity, simply stated, is recognizing and celebrating our differences in society and acknowledging the contributions of multicultural groups to the fabric that is America. We began by offering diverse examples in instruction: the Harlem Renaissance as an example of American literature, Chicano muralists when covering contemporary American artists, Executive Order 9066 (the American concentration camps) or water rights and Indian lands when teaching American history. As more classes began requiring ethnic/cultural diversity research; the team teaching model also enabled us to teach one another about ethnic studies reference materials.

Many freshman English writing classes requested library

instruction that would introduce students to basic library services and sources to research their family history from a social
issues perspective. Specifically, their final papers were to discuss not only what the United States of America was like when
their families immigrated here, but the whys and hows of their
decisions to come. The paper concluded by describing these
events and its positive and/or negative impact on their lives.
This teaching opportunity was a chance to not only do "show
and tell" with some of the cultural resources available (e.g. Harvard Encyclopedia of American Ethnic Groups) but to actually
raise some eyebrows (including our own)! Two of us agreed
to begin the session with a piece read aloud from the Ethnic
Almanac entitled, "Gee, You Don't Look Puerto Rican," written by Irma Alvarado[4]. It tells the story of a Puerto Rican woman
growing up in New York who learned at a very early age that
it was "wrong" to be Puerto Rican. She would disguise her
true ethnic identity by claiming her people were directly from
Spain or South America, anywhere but Puerto Rico. Fortunately
over time, Irma learned it was better for her to identify with
her ethnic heritage. This short piece (which took less than five
minutes to read) probably stayed with many of the students
much longer and provided them with something they weren't
expecting from "yet another" library lecture; it realistically introduced them to some of the questions and issues they very
well might encounter in their own research.

FURTHER DOWNSIZING AND DIVERSIFYING

The concept of downsizing needs no introduction to this
audience—we have heard of budget and staff reductions in
higher education accompanied by the flattening of the academic
organization to cope with diminishing resources. The libraries
of the University of California are no exception; staffing levels
had been reduced by a succession of early retirement programs,
normal job attrition and a downsizing program that left many
vacant positions unfilled. At UCSB, the Library attacked this
problem by combining two reference desks and their collections:
Government Publications and Main Reference became Human-

ities/Social Sciences Reference Desk and the librarians became
the Reference Services Group. Coordinators for various reference functions were appointed to manage the activities of the
group, resulting in a less hierarchical organizational structure.
With the exception of the Humanities/Social Sciences Reference
Desk Coordinator who was responsible for the reference collection and the scheduling of the reference desk, responsibilities for the coordinator positions extended library-wide to cover
the following areas: computerized information services, the information desk, LAN information access, library publications
(user guides and library signs), training, and user instruction.
Coordinators for ethnic, gender and area studies, humanities,
preservation, sciences, and social sciences collections were also
appointed.

Merging the two departments and their reference collections meant all librarians needed to be cross-trained on new
reference materials and paging procedures. Many training sessions on various subject specialties were held during the summer before the start of the academic year. One approach to
expose and familiarize librarians to reference options in the humanities, social sciences, and ethnic studies materials was to
combine subject training into possible interdisciplinary research
questions. "Read the Book, See the Movie" was the name of
the training class which combined the related subject areas of
literature and film studies research. Chicano and Latin American Studies, unique disciplines with overlapping resources, was
another session. Business and economics reference training was
supplemented with government and international documents.
These are just a few examples of the training sessions presented last summer.

Library instruction had taken place on two different levels: librarian-student, librarian-librarian. The traditional bibliographic instruction model was expanded to include faculty.
Working with the faculty who assigned effective library assignments and who strongly supported library instruction further
validated collection development in diverse areas for the reference and circulating collections. Dynamic, interdisciplinary
library instruction was motivating many of the faculty to develop innovative assignments and courses. In librarian-student

instruction we demonstrated the use of print materials in combination with computerized resources including examples of cultural diversity acquired through the earlier librarian cross training. This became a very successful strategy as the Freshman English Writing Program was focusing more on contemporary social issues and away from the traditional literary criticism. Another benefit gained from this outreach was that the library and its librarians became more visible to the academic community. The faculty began to work more with us in developing new courses and we, in turn, were modifying their view of traditional library instruction and library resources.

CONCLUSION

Downsizing and diversifying our roles as instructors while being aware that cultural diversity exists, is an ongoing process. We continue to team-teach, give interactive professional training, and do faculty outreach through our bibliographic instruction. Downsizing, in effect, has produced a situation where all of us, regardless of specialization, are being faced with diversity on one level or another. It is our aim not to stay conscious of the "other" as we downsize and diversify, while at the same time recognizing the many backgrounds and experiences we all bring to every class.

In her article, "Multiculturalism: Beyond Sushi and Enchiladas," Mei Nakano's response to the question "Why are we always talking about the differences between us?"

Of course we have similarities. We are, after all, the same species with the same basic needs, drives and aspirations, and we do share some basic values. But we are different in significant ways. Look at me. My face is different from yours. And based on what that has meant in this society, my experience in the same environment in which you live has been different. Rather than ignore that, I would hope that you and I could look at each other, recognize the differences and learn to appreciate them.

ENDNOTES

1. Cultural Diversity in Undergraduate Education: What's Working, What Could Work. Conference held April 1989, Irvine, California.

2. See Joseph A. Boisse and Connie V. Dowell, "Increasing Minority Librarians in Academic Research Libraries," Library Journal, 112 (7) April 15, 1987:52.

3. See Cheryl LaGuardia, et al., "Learning to Instruct on the Job: Team-Teaching Library Skills," Reference Librarian, 40 (1993): 53-62.

4. Bernardo, Stephanie. The Ethnic Almanac (Garden City, NY: Doubleday & Co., 1981), 130. Nakano, Mei. "Multiculturalism: Beyond Sushi and Enchiladas," Pacific Citizen, –2740/vol 118 no. 4 (February 4-10, 1994):5

17

Successful Research Using the Gateway to Information: Meeting the Challenge of User Independence

Fred Roecker
Ohio State University

BIBLIOGRAPHIC INSTRUCTION AT OHIO STATE

User Education and bibliographic instruction (BI) have been a part of The Ohio State University Libraries for 16 years. Over 35,000 students each year receive some form of BI assistance on electronic databases, course-related instruction, or an introduction to research. All 10,000 new freshmen and transfer sophomores receive a presentation on research and then complete two required library assignments. Orientation sessions for international students are offered quarterly. BI classes are also taught by Ohio State librarians to satisfy faculty tenure requirements. Reference BI help is available in all libraries, as well as a desk staffed with volunteers in the Main Library who assist users with our notoriously hostile online catalog, LCS.

The overall goal of the Office of Library User Education is to make independent, successful information users out of people with library needs. The search strategy concept is at the core of this goal and is found in most BI sessions. Ohio State students beginning a research project face 26 department libraries, 20 special library collections, 4.5 million books, and 30,000 periodical subscriptions. They are often overwhelmed and need a systematic approach to resolve their information need. To address this, we have relied on the search strategy concept to give an overview of important research materials and present a logical pathway to search in an organized manner. Users following the search strategy move from broad, background resources such as encyclopedias, through current information in indexes and the online catalog, and then on to more specialized materials containing statistical, biographical, and review information.

EVALUATION OF THE USER
EDUCATION PROGRAM

In the mid-1980's Virginia Tiefil, head of Library User Education, evaluated the existing User Ed program. Nearly half of the 54,000 students were not receiving BI. The new resources available and the changing nature of information made even those students attending one workshop unable to be considered "information literate." She also noted that library workshop attendance had recently dropped significantly, despite User Education Office efforts to boost attendance through different topics, times, and formats.

While research help was available in the Libraries at the reference desk, increasing numbers of students were beginning to conduct their research from home, offices, computer labs, and dorms, or in the evenings when few of the department library reference desks were staffed. Continuing Education students and remote users looked for point-of-need assistance whenever they searched for library materials, whether in a library or as a remote user. They wanted to sit down and immediately understand how to find materials, and search research databases, and if a problem arose, to find a clear, handy point-of-need instructions (brochures or people).

LIMITED OPTIONS

User Education set out to address the research habits of these users. More workshops could be offered, but would anyone come given the changing attitude of users? Also, the three User Ed librarians (and other University Libraries' staff) could not expand their teaching load and still maintain their assigned responsibilities. The library budget, of course, did not have funds available for hiring more User Ed Office personnel.

Because workshops were not the answer, other options were considered. More instructional brochures could be created, but they were time-consuming to develop, costly to print, needed constant revision, and users did not seem to retain the information these instructional materials provided. More reference staff could assist users at point-of-need, but the budget was forcing decreases in staffing and shortening library hours. Other BI options could be tried, but there was little University Libraries' money available for new projects.

THE IDEA OF THE GATEWAY

Tiefil felt that BI at Ohio State had to become less dependent on workshops, brochures, and even staff help. The basic and changing information-seeking needs of the user remained unchanged and had to be addressed. Users still needed to understand a search strategy, how to focus their topic, and to identify, locate, and evaluate broad and focused resources. They needed to be able to select and successfully search a variety of databases. And they needed to understand the University Libraries system and the relevant circulation procedures.

Tiefil felt because workshops could no longer convey this

information, a computer might be an answer. Computers could be available both in libraries and remotely. They could present the search strategy concept and guide users to relevant materials. Electronic resources could be frontended and linked to every computer to simplify database searching. University Library information such as floor plans, maps, hours, policies, and anything else relevant could be included. Ideally, any such computer system had to be easy enough to use that workshops, brochures, or staff assistance would never be required for successful searching.

Tiefel's aim was always to enable students to be independent information users. Instead of listening in a workshop or practicing on a CAI terminal, users would find materials and BI assistance from one location when they needed it. Brochures would not be necessary because screens would be clear even to novice computer users. Staff could then help users with more complex research problems, knowing users were finding the core materials and answering basic reference questions through the computer system.

DEVELOPING THE PROTOTYPE

Any funding for such a system would have to come from grants. In 1987 the Fund for the Improvement for Post-Secondary Education (FIPSE) showed their belief in the idea and gave the project a $170,000 three year grant to get started. Other money over the next five years came from two Department of Education Title IID grants and one from the William Randolph Hearst Foundation, totaling about a half-million dollars ($1.5 million). During this time, the University Libraries contributed staff time valued at approximately one-half million dollars, as well as some computer and network equipment.

Once funded, as the first step to develop the project, User Ed sought ideas from library staff to involve the many library, design, and technical interest groups at Ohio State. The Office of Library Automation under Susan Logan coordinated all technical development. Committees composed of library staff gave input on design and technology, while consultants from both on and off-campus were enlisted to guide the overall development. A Programmer/Analyst was hired along with two student workers to develop the software and assemble the hardware. Nancy O'Hanlon, head of the Undergraduate Library Reference Department, pulled the diverse ideas from these groups together to develop a consistent format and determine content guidelines. All this was started in 1987 and, by summer 1989, the first prototype all-in-one library computer system was created, called The Gateway to Information.

FIRST LOCATIONS

The early prototypes were evaluated by library staff and faculty on a single workstation in a closed-off faculty area. Later, test groups of freshmen were asked to answer specific reference questions using only The Gateway. Sample questions included "What are three indexes for finding articles that deal with motion pictures?" "In what ways is LCS different from the card catalog?" "Where is the Map Collection located?" etc. The programmers and User Ed librarians observed and questioned students closely regarding their impressions of the system, and then worked to modify the screen content and functionality to address the user's problems and suggestions. User Ed librarians worked on the content and design while the Automation Office modified the technology. This cooperation between library departments ensured a product that would be user-friendly, effective, and powerful.

Two workstations were introduced in a public area for testing in January 1990. Workstations were opened for a few hours daily with a User Ed librarian observing all users and asking for comments. In July of that year, two more workstations were added and left unattended in the Main Library. By 1991, the last four computers provided for in the grant were added to the Undergraduate Library, bringing the total number of workstations to eight in two locations. Additional workstations would have to come from the Libraries' budget.

USER-DRIVEN PROJECT

It became clear that additional funding could now only be obtained by proving to granting agencies and the Libraries' administration that The Gateway was working and that users considered it valuable. And so, evaluating the system became a permanent feature of The Gateway. Evaluation forms were placed by each workstation, collected and then compiled monthly for administrators and developers to hear and act on suggestions and shortcomings.

Users made it clear what they wanted: less text and more direct access to materials, and full text if possible. The campus maps and floor plans were a big hit, as was the simplified, common front end to LCS and the eight Wilson databases. (We selected Wilson for their coverage of core subjects and also because they did not charge a site license to network their databases.) Grolier's Electronic Encyclopedia provided the full text materials users desired and was heavily used. User statistics and comments guided The Gateway development from being a BI workstation with lots of explanatory text to an access computer that speeded people to information about relevant items and let them search electronic versions where available.

BASED ON THE SEARCH STRATEGY

The search strategy diagram was used as the opening screen. It illustrated pathways users could consider to quickly find known titles, be guided to relevant materials, or receive BI information if desired on organizing research and core materials used for specific needs.

Users could learn when to use an encyclopedia, or even a specialized encyclopedia. Certain indexes had electronic versions and these electronic indexes could be searched by subject or three keywords. (Full functionality was not available as it was too time-consuming and costly to program in the first versions.) They found periodical indexes on 90 subjects, saw that some had abstracts and others did not. And according to Circulation Department statistics, users understood how to search for books and then check out or save desired titles using LCS, an understanding that previously required 40,000 instructional brochures per year, dozens of workshops, and constant staff assistance.

HOW IT WORKS

Macintosh was selected as the platform for The Gateway because HyperCard software was very easy to program and update, it supported graphics, and it was free with each Apple computer purchased. The workstation requirements were Class II or better (LC, Si, CX, etc.) with a 12" screen, the latter decision reached after the Library Director mentioned how difficult the small-screen Macs were to use. Color monitors were not needed since HyperCard then did not support color.

The Gateway consists of a series of HyperCard screen connected to the first screen, a map of the Search Strategy. Users can quickly see the variety of resources such as encyclopedias, periodical indexes, statistics, reviews, etc., available in Ohio State Libraries and read descriptions for the contents and possible uses for each resource type. There are pathways for those who are unsure what they want to use and even pathways containing ideas for research assignments. Clicking the mouse on a button takes users to any desired area.

If a user decides the best resource is an electronic database, The Gateway allows him to access it by clicking on a "Search This Index" button. This opens a telnet connection which links the public workstation through our local network (SONNET) and on to the networked resources. The database can be our online catalog or one of 20 CD-ROMs mounted in the Library. Mac TCP software allows the Macintosh computer to read DOS databases such as the CD-ROMs and LCS.

Whether a Wilson, UMI, SilverPlatter, or Grolier database or our LCS catalog, users are presented with a common, user-friendly interface and command language that helps even the first time user successfully search any database. MitemView software allows programmers to customize the display of the DOS information onto a HyperCard template screen.

Gateway users can also search remote Internet catalog or OhioLINK (the centralized catalog of 18 Ohio Libraries and informational databases such as ABI Inform and General Periodicals Index located in Dayton about 50 miles from Columbus. Yet with The Gateway, these and any other Internet resources can be accessed as quickly as the databases mounted in the Main Library.

EXPANSION THROUGHOUT
THE UNIVERSITY LIBRARIES

By 1992, only the eight grantfunded workstations were available in two University Libraries. Evaluations were consistently favorable, and we reached a turning point in the project. For The Gateway to survive, it had to become the major computer workstation in the Libraries. The few grant-funded computers could easily be overlooked by students. Gateway grant moneys were near their end. The programming costs for only a few workstations could become a low priority for the Automation Office. We feared the project would be neglected into oblivion. Only if it replaced the existing LCS terminals in all department libraries could The Gateway hope to gain permanent use by student users and, more importantly, gain funding and long-term commitments from the Libraries.

The Gateway had two strong factors in its favor to become the single library workstation at Ohio State. First, the University Libraries' 100 LCS Telex terminals were worn out, and funds were already in the budget to replace them. But other computer costs had to be considered before purchasing any replacements. The Libraries pay a monthly fee for each port to the online catalog. Each Telex terminal required one LCS port. One of the first methods to save the Libraries' money had been to cut the 100 public computer terminals (and thus the required ports) to 50. With fewer ports available, a microcomputer that allowed sharing of ports was more desirable over a hard-wired (directly-linked) dumb terminal. Microcomputers would allow the sharing of ports and thus require fewer ports to support more workstations. Remote searching from dorms, labs, and office would also be possible with a networked microcomputer. The Gateway having operated in a networked environment for two years, was a seasoned performer in the areas desired by the library administration.

A DOS computer could also accomplish this sharing of LCS ports and networking of CD-ROMs just like the Gateway Macintosh. But with two years in the public and 3,000 evaluations from users who had achieved success in their research, The Gateway justified its usefulness to students. (One additional factor in favor of The Gateway was that in January 1992 Apple had a huge sale on the Mac IISi computers, the workstation which could deliver The Gateway program.)

The University Libraries committed to The Gateway and purchased 50 Macintosh microcomputers to replace all the Telex dumb terminals in all Libraries. Eventually, 20 more Macs were added to create a Gateway computer lab in the Undergraduate Library to meet the needs of the 10,000-student Freshmen using The Gateway for two library assignments. All of this was possible despite the downsized environment at Ohio State because of the successful performance record over two years as demonstrated through thousands of user evaluations.

The Office of User Education also contributed to making The Gateway a permanent research tool at Ohio State. They gave up one of their faculty positions to make funds available for the Libraries to hire a full-time programmer for the project who would report to the Automation Office.

CURRENT EVALUATIONS

Recent evaluations from 460 users in January 1994 show that 82% consider their success on The Gateway "completely" or "mostly successful." Screens were rated "Very" or "mostly clear" by 90% of users, and 54% found "much more" or "more" information than searching using other research methods. The Gateway was considered "very" or "mostly easy" to use by 83%.

One of the concerns of Gateway developers was that narrative pathways and resources would be considered too basic by upper level and graduate students. Statistics taken from 5,000 evaluations over the period of July 16, 1990 (when The Gateway was first left unattended) to December 31, 1993, however, show that 46% of users are senior or graduate students, with 34% freshmen, sophomores, and juniors.

Library Administrators were concerned about the small number of workstations available. With the variety of resources to be found and searched on The Gateway, they feared users stay at computers for long periods of time, causing long lines of frustrated users. Statistics from January 1994 indicated that 62% spent less than 20 minutes on the computer (25% spent less than 10 minutes), and 20% spend between 20 and 40 minutes. Only 14% of users spent more than 40 minutes doing research on The Gateway. There still are occasional lines at peak times of the day during midquarter, but this problem can only be solved with more computers or making The Gateway available from non-library locations.

REMOTE EXPANSION

As of winter 1994, The Gateway is not yet available over the Internet. Licensing restrictions from CD-ROM vendors limit access to the Ohio State Libraries and computer labs. Also, graphics do not travel over the network easily.

However, The Gateway has moved to a client/server platform, with one computer (the "server") maintaining the narrative screen text and directing database searching requests from all Gateway workstations (the "clients") to the proper database locations in the CD-ROM tower, LCS mainframe computer, or remote catalogs. Maintenance is done centrally to the server and automatically updated daily to the eighty individual hard drives. This client/server format will facilitate remote searching as users will have their computer/clients access the server rather than store all narrative text and technology on their computers.

THE FUTURE

We are confident The Gateway's narrative, search strategy, and overall design are applicable to any library. Libraries facing the same downsizing restrictions of fewer staff, shorter reference hours, cutbacks in brochures, workshops, and public workstations, will be looking into some type of system that makes library research easier for users, inexpensive for administrators, and staff-friendly for librarians. Even if circumstances did not require downsizing, The Gateway is effective because it has been designed to address users' needs.

The Gateway has been successfully transferred to The University of Cincinnati for demonstration at EDUCOM 1993. They merely updated the titles and narrative source cards to reflect their holdings, created new floor plans and maps, and linked their online catalog and CD-ROM databases into the narrative.

Ohio State is not pursuing marketing of The Gateway at this time, but is looking into expansion on the campus as the first priority. Another exciting possibility is mounting The Gateway onto Mosaic software. This will immediately make it available on any computer with tremendous expansion of functionality, including color, down-loaded pictures, sound, and multimedia.

CONCLUSIONS

The Gateway to Information came into the Ohio State Libraries during a crisis time when the budget was slashed, hours shortened, and BI assistance cut back. User education was needed more than ever to help users deal with the growing variety and complexity of electronic and print materials in a major research facility. The Gateway was born because of a crisis: addressing the on-going user needs when the Libraries were severely restricted in their services.

The one-stop shopping workstation Virginia Tiefel dreamed of in the 1980s is now an integral part of research in the University Libraries. Users accept them as essential for answering many of their core research needs. Users are successfully being lead to relevant materials regardless of format, even when no reference librarians are available. Electronic databases such as Applied Science and Technology, Biological Abstracts, ERIC, and Essay and General Literature Index are no longer a mystery requiring complex search commands. Users can easily do keyword searches to locate relevant articles, search for the found journals in LCS, find maps and floor plans to the libraries holding the items, and print the results of their searches . . . all from one workstation. And it needs no workshops, instructional brochures, or staff assistance.

18

Managing the Three-Ring Circus: A Case Study of Collaborative Teaching and Learning in the Large Lecture Format

Dr. Deborah Petersen-Perlman and Dr. Marilyn Russell-Bogle
University of Minnesota, Duluth

Petersen-Perlman, Professor:

As a student, I have clear memories of the dark, anonymous comfort of the mass lecture class. Sitting in the back row of an auditorium with the lights dimmed and the lecturer droning on and on, it didn't really matter to anyone whether or not I was there, nor did it matter whether or not I paid attention. God forbid anyone should call on me. I liked being a number in this one class, even if my other classes were much more

Editorial Note: This paper as originally delivered was written mostly from the pedagogical point of view of a professor teaching in a large lecture class. For reasons of manuscript size and audience, it has been substantially edited to focus on the librarian's role in working with these classes.

intimate. This was the one class I could cut with impunity (as long as I obtained lecture notes from someone else). Years passed and then, the shoe appeared on the other foot. I was the professor, and there I was—faced with that anonymous mass of students who were as clearly indifferent to my class as I had been to my mass lecture classes.

As a teacher who loves what she does, I clearly do not want students to have the attitude I had in this long-ago mass lecture. I also believe in employing a variety of teaching approaches to each class. These goals are greatly impeded by the large lecture format. Large lecture classes are frequently freshman-oriented survey classes which can be used to fulfill liberal education requirements, and/or to serve as a prerequisite for a major. The job is too big to be handled alone. Thus I believe in the power of collaboration.

There are days when I am simply not ''up'' to the old dog and pony show. I knew that I could carry off the stand-up act from time to time, but I also knew there would be days when the only thing that would work to my satisfaction would be good old fashioned class-interaction. Holding a discussion or other small group sessions in a lecture hall seemed to be rather oxymoronic, but I knew from my own pedagogical preferences that I wanted that contact with my students, and I knew I was going to have to break down some rather formidable barriers in order to achieve my goals.

Journalism 1100—Introduction to Mass Communication—serves as one of three prerequisites for the Communication major at the University of Minnesota, Duluth. Students interested in pursuing the Communication major need to receive a C or better. This course also fulfills 3 credits of the social science category of the Liberal Education program.

From the outset, the course has a few strikes against it. As a prerequisite to the major, many precommunication students feel the pressure of receiving a good grade. Other students select the course as the least objectionable option with which to fulfill Liberal Education credits. Some are actually interested in the subject matter, but they anticipate instruction in journalistic writing and are disappointed when they realize that they are writing abstracts and analytical essays rather than journalistic articles (in spite of catalogue copy which identifies the survey nature of the course). The course is usually very large, attracting between 130 and 200 students. To accommodate a class with this many students the university schedules the course for a large lecture hall with fixed seating. The classroom is very traditionally and rigidly structured; it is not a conducive environment for small group interaction. One of my primary tasks is to break down these structural barriers by encouraging independent writing, small group work, and general class discussions.

I wanted to make the course more inclusive of the wide variety of student learning styles and interests within the class and I knew I needed help to accomplish that goal. I sought out assistance from the Instructional Development Service [hereafter referred to as IDS], a consultative body within our institution, the function of which is to assist professors with developing teaching skills (while I will make reference to IDS and other agents with whom I collaborated throughout the paper, I will focus on the collaborative process more specifically under Ring 3).

RING #1: INCLASS ACTIVITIES

There is only a small coterie of students who volunteer contributions on a regular basis. These few participants are looked on as ''overactive deviants'' by the larger body. Their frequent comments are resented by the more reticent students.

In my efforts to monitor the success or failure of different efforts within the classroom I consulted an IDS consultant. My consultant served as an observer and analyst. The IDS consultant and I agreed that it was extremely important to invite more students into the discussion.

I encouraged active participation by as many students as possible through a number of different writing strategies. One technique, discovery writing, encourages students to write impromptu essays on topics which have been covered in assigned readings. The end-of-class summary and reflection version of discovery writing is a technique called the ''one-minute paper,'' described by Patricia Cross. Both writing exercises require ac-

tive debriefing, which takes the form of preliminary class discussion at the beginning of the next class session. The one
minute paper offers the professor a check on individual class
sessions and can provide opportunities for review and clarifi-
cation.

RING #2: ACTIVITIES OUTSIDE OF THE CLASS

Kolb (quoted in Svinicki & Dixon, 1987) suggests four different learner types which he claims exist in all classrooms: the
diverger, the assimilator, the converger, and the accommoda-
tor. The activities described in Ring #1 required reflection and
abstract conceptualization. It was clear that not all students
thrived within those kinds of experiences. In Ring #2, I worked
at designing exercises which were more directed at concrete
and active experimentation learners.

I attempted to reach out to these different learners in a
group-based assignment which I designed to supplement the
text and in-class discussions. Because mine was a class focused
on the media, I conceived of an assignment which required students to pay an onsite visit to a local media outlet (of the student's choosing) and to attend to the employment and editorial
practices and policies of each location. The students visited in
teams and then reported back to the class (as a team) on what
they had discovered. I offered a template of questions they were
required to address, and I suggested standards for grades of
A, B, and C. I indicated that the quality of the presentations
would be enhanced by audio/visual aids (such as music, slides,
overheads, videos, etc.). Much to my personal disappointment,
the assignment was something of a bust. Unfortunately, it took
on a sophomoric air (somewhat like a High School field trip,
instead of the participant/observation experience I had envisioned). The presentations ended up being rather pedantic
and redundant. Furthermore, while some students did take the
assignment seriously, others rode on the coat tails of their more
ambitious colleagues. In other words, this project suffered from
all of the problems which attend group work in general. After
two quarters I abandoned this assignment. I do believe this
could have been managed more effectively. I sought assistance
from the librarian assigned to my area.

Russell-Bogle, Librarian:
To facilitate the professor's goals concerning active and concrete learning experiences, I shared the following "Principles of Collaborative Learning."

1. Principle of heterogeneous grouping:
mix groups according to "real world";
mix different skill levels, gender, ethnicity, physical abilities, etc.;
teach students to work with "different" types of persons.

2. Principle of positive interdependence:
individual accountability/individual rewards;
group accountability/group rewards;
students taught to recognize and value dependence of group;
students taught negotiation skills to work for overall goals;
more creative and diverse ideas can be generated by a group.

3. Principle of social skills acquisition:
acquiring positive social skills is vital to one's education;
positive and appropriate social skills can be learned;
there are various types of social skills (ethnic, school, social, etc.).

4. Principle of distributed leadership:
students are capable of understanding, learning, performing leadership tasks;
students become more active participants when leadership roles are expected from them leadership roles should be rotated among members of the group.

5. Principle of group autonomy:
students will resolve most problems if they know that the teacher will not routinely rescue them;
students are also sources of information;
students are capable of teaching each other.

Petersen-Perlman:
I should have striven to achieve a "real world" mix in class groups and I should have specified the nature of individual responsibility by assigning individual tasks to each group par-

ticipant. Furthermore, I should have rotated leadership responsibilities as suggested in these Principles for Collaborative Learning. Finally, I should have taken pains to instruct the students
in negotiation skills. Collaboration with the librarian on this assignment has produced a more effective assignment design for
future class sessions.

At the same time I introduced media on-site visitations and
reports. Also I instituted an alternative assignment for students
who did not like working in groups. Students were asked to
select an issue of public importance and to follow the media
coverage of that issue for the duration of the quarter. They were
to submit annotated bibliography entries on media coverage
of their selected issue. I informed them that they could con-
tract for different grades on this particular assignment:

- a C was a simple summary;
- a B represented analysis based on questions dealing with
  consistency, position of the article, credibility of the source,
  and assessment of the article's balance/objectivity/fairness;
- an A required original insight, synthesis of all the entries,
  and integration of what was learned in class with what the
  students had learned by doing the project.

I wanted to encourage students to develop research skills.
I had two, additional pedagogical objectives in making this assignment. My first goal was to expose students to a variety of
media which they might not otherwise encounter. Secondly,
I wanted to help students develop critical thinking skills by
evaluating the material they encountered according to issues
of credibility, bias, accuracy, and consistency. I wanted the students to watch, listen, and read clearly identifiable political
media from special interest groups, the foreign press, representatives of the American political left and the right, as well as
the more mainstream media. To that end I invited my colleague
from the library to offer two class sessions on critical thinking
and bibliographic instruction. She offered the students a systematic procedure for tracking down sources through both electronic and paper indices. She then assisted them, through an
inclass exercise, in making evaluative judgments about the articles they were going to read.

Russell-Bogle: *On Critical Thinking*
and Bibliographic Instruction:
My understanding of critical thinking is that it involves educating students to use an exploratory process for the task of learning something. The instructor presents a subject and stimulates the student to explore it. The next step is for the student to consolidate what he or she found into some sort of concept and then apply this to a new related problem.

A lot has been written about critical thinking, including some articles about librarians and their role in teaching critical thinking. The literature suggests that we begin with the premise that one first needs subject knowledge, then skills to update that knowledge with new information. How then do librarians fit in here, or do they? One writer, Eugene Engeldinger, states that librarians are willing to provide partial solutions to this problem and most are willing to help instruct students in how to find information. But helping students determine the quality of the information, or to evaluate a particular item, is often left up to someone else, usually the classroom instructor. How do we as librarians feel about this? What do we consider our role to be in helping students learn critical thinking? Should we consider it our responsibility to teach students to think critically?

Is the ability to think critically necessary to the development of independence and competence for an adult, and is thinking critically the mark of an educated person? Soni Bodi suggests that because of our rapidly changing society, certain kinds of information will become obsolete, and knowing HOW to think has become as important as knowing WHAT to think. She goes on to state that learning to think critically is, in large measure, learning what sorts of questions to ask and when to ask them, and then knowing how much evidence is enough to determine the validity of a statement. Because critical thinking is not a universal skill, it should be taught as an integral part of a subject. How then can librarians encourage and reinforce what is being done in the classroom? We, as librarians, need to go beyond the ''how to'' of searching for information to address the uses to which information can be put once it has been found.

Critical thinking is not a new pedagogical term. Classic definitions of critical thinking have been developed by John Dewey, Benjamin Bloom, D.A. Kolb, and Jean Piaget, just to name a few.

Dewey's concept of reflective thinking suggests five states of thinking: 1) suggestions, in which the mind leaps forward to a possible solution; 2) an intellectualization of the difficulty that has been felt into a problem to be solved, a question for which the answer must be sought; 3) the use of one suggestion after another as a leading idea, or hypothesis, to initiate and guide observation and other operations in collection of factual material; 4) the mental elaboration of the idea; and 5) testing the hypothesis by overt or imaginative action.

Benjamin Bloom's taxonomy of cognitive skills identifies three types of classification of objectives: cognitive, affective, and psychomotor. The existence of such a classification system tended to focus discussion of educational objectives on whether schools should have responsibility for objectives in the affective domain (interests, attitudes, appreciations) or whether their primary focus should be on the cognitive domain. Cognitive science research on thinking has centered on problem solving. Kinds of situations labeled "problem solving" require putting together a novel sequence of processes to achieve a goal.

D.A. Kolb drew upon the tradition of Dewey and developed the concept of a learning cycle that circles from a basis of concrete experience to observations and reflection, which are assimilated into the formation of abstract concepts and generalizations, which lead to the drawing and testing of implications to the concepts in new situations.

Jean Piaget, a psychologist, developed a theory of how intellectual functioning is qualitatively different at different ages and how the student needs interaction with the environment to gain intellectual competence. Piaget's cognitive development theory focused on four principles: 1) to know is to act, that students are the architects of their own knowledge and intelligence; 2) education should be student centered; 3) education should be individualized; and 4) social interaction should play a significant role in the classroom.

The central idea in Piaget's Theory is that logic develops. There are three major periods in this development of logic;

1) sensory-motor period, 2) concrete operations period and 3) formal operations period.

In order to define critical thinking, we also need to discover what it is not. Critical thinking is not necessarily synonymous with creative thinking, problem solving, or logic, although each of these abilities is part of critical thinking. Creative thinking does not involve a process of evaluation as critical thinking does, but critical thinking does include creative thinking. Critical thinking involves more than problem solving; problem solving is a progressively narrowing process while critical thinking is an expanding, exploratory process. And critical thinking is not the same as logical thinking. Finding the fallacies in logic is only a part of critical thinking, and logic cannot generate theories or arguments.

How do we then define critical thinking? A few definitions are:

1. It is the process of determining authenticity, accuracy, and worth of information or knowledge claims or arguments (Beyer, 1985).
2. It is the evaluation of evidence based upon acceptable standards (Freeley, 1985).
3. It is the ability to evaluate different perspectives and challenge assumptions.
4. It is to learn, to make informed decisions, to evaluate applications of knowledge, and to find truth.
5. It is related to subject knowledge.
6. It is reflective and reasonable thinking that focuses on deciding what to believe or do (Ennis, 1985).
7. It comprises the mental process, strategies, and representations people use to solve problems, make decisions, and learn new concepts (Sternberg, 1985).
8. It is an individual engaged in mediating a problem, rather than learning through the stimulus-response mode.

Nancy Thomas Totten suggests that almost all definitions include the concepts of analyzing and evaluating information, which imply the ability to: 1) assess reliability of a source, 2) distinguish between fact and opinion, 3) identify hidden assumptions, and 4) recognize bias, logical fallacy, and ir-relevance.

The difference comes into play when you consider whether critical thinking is taught within a subject specific discipline or as a nondisciplinary approach. The generalist approach to teach-ing critical thinking skills has some problems. According to Nancy Thomas Totten, one of these is the problem of estab-lishing standards and skills not tied to a discipline. A second problem relates to the attitudes and stage of intellectual develop-ment of the students. She goes on to state that programs should allow for active student participation, teacher encouragement, and student-to-student interaction.

It is important for academic librarians to provide instruc-tion and guidance to students for critically evaluating informa-tion and information sources. This is most appropriate when the need arises. We should continue to develop our own ap-proaches, both discipline specific approaches and general ap-proaches as well. We need to be aware of incorporating all modes of thinking into the process: that creative thinking and logical thinking have a place in critical thinking skills. It is im-portant to incorporate the skills which enable the reasoner to analyze logically and evaluate problems, and to use the pat-tern of discovery skills to promote the creative construction of alternative ideas and the imaginative discovery of new problems and fresh perspectives.

Applying these concepts of critical thinking and bibliograph-ic instruction to the journalism class resulted in the formula-tion of the following set of questions which I termed "Systematic Evaluation of Journalistic Writing."

1. Who is the author?
   a. What is the author's experience?
   b. What are the author's qualifications?
2. What is the author's purpose in writing this article?
3. Who is the intended audience/what is the nature of this publication?
   a. Is this a general periodical/readership?
   b. Is this a specialized journal/professional readership?
4. Is the style of the article related to the nature of the publi-cation? If so, how so?

5. Does the author have a bias?
6. Is the author operating from a clear set of assumptions about the readership?
7. What data collection method did the author use?
   a. Does the author employ personal opinion/commentary? If so, how much?
   b. Has the author engaged in systematic research? What is the author's methodology?
   c. Did the author employ tests to measure assumptions?
8. What are the author's conclusions?
   a. Are these conclusions justified?
   b. Why or why not?
9. Is the material in the article consistent with other information you have read on the same topic?
   a. In what ways is it similar?
   b. In what ways is it different?
   c. To what factors do you attribute these similarities and differences?
10. Are there important attachments to this article (bibliographies, highlight boxes, tables, graphs, charts, etc.)? If there aren't, should there be?

Petersen-Perlman:
While students complained about the amount of time this project required, since I implemented it I have had many students tell me it was one of the most important experiences of their college careers. In an anonymous survey of student attitudes toward class assignments, 72% identified the annotation assignment as helpful. I am proud to say that when the assignment coincided with the 1992 presidential campaign, 85% of those students who were of voting age in the class cast their votes in the election and did so on the basis of information they had collected as a function of their assignment.

RING #3: LIBRARY COLLABORATION

In preparing this class I have always found it helpful to meet with the librarians assigned to my area so as to determine what resources will be available to my students. For example, some years back I determined that I wanted my students to follow events as they transpired in the former Soviet Union. After meeting with my area librarian I decided that such a focus would be futile and frustrating for all involved. The time delay in receiving relevant materials would be too great to provide for the kind of depth and diversity my assignments required. This consultation resulted in a more manageable assignment for the students and the librarians alike.

Additionally, I have found it valuable to run through mock assignments with the librarians to make sure that the assignments I have made can be done with ease. It's valuable to go through the experience you expect your students to have. From the librarian's perspective, such trial runs can facilitate their bibliographic instruction responsibilities. Once they have become familiar with what the professor is requiring they can point students in the right direction and engage in one-on-one learning which extends instruction beyond the classroom doors.

CONCLUSION

This case represents an anomaly in many regards. Not everyone who teaches large lecture classes is going to have the energy (psychic and physical) necessary to teach in this particular manner. Furthermore, the investment in time is extraordinary and clearly represents a sacrifice. Finally, one must be creative in amassing resources to facilitate effective instruction of the kind described. In particular, one must be alert to assistance possibilities among both students and staff. This kind of teaching requires organization and structure akin to that required of the circus ringmaster. The teacher, like the ringmaster, must coordinate multiple activities and concerns simultaneously.

Today, teaching takes place through many media: lectures, seminars, workshops, laboratories, individualized instruction, collaborative teaching, and even the application of new technologies. The curriculum is a reflection of the ever-expanding body of knowledge that is out there and continues to be in flux. Throughout its evolution, there have always been questions of balance: the balance between theory and practice, integration and fragmentation, the past and the future, breadth and depth, institutional requirements and student and teacher choices.

Student learning not only results from teaching and the nature of curriculum, but is also influenced by out-of-class interaction with faculty, academic colleagues, other students, and experiential learning. The circus big top can be a scary place, but it is also one of the most exciting and memorable environments one is likely to experience.

BIBLIOGRAPHY

Cannon, L.W. (1990). Fostering positive race, class, and gender dynamics in the classroom. Women's Studies Quarterly 1990: 1 & 2, 126-134.

Hilsen, L.R. (1992, Spring). Transforming teaching: Hearing all the voices. Instructional Development IX: 3, 3 & 6-8.

Krupnick, C.G. (1985). Women and men in the classroom: Inequality and its remedies. Teaching and Learning, 1: 1, 18-25.

Krupnick, C.G. (1991, March). Learnings from co-education: Issues and research on women and men on campus. Session presented at the Harvard University Graduate School of Education Conference on Women and Men on Campus: Inequality and Its Remedies, Cambridge, MA.

Light, R.J. (1990). The Harvard assessment seminars first report, 1990: Explorations with students and faculty about teaching, learning, and student life. Cambridge, MA: Harvard University Graduate School of Education and Kennedy School of Government.

Petersen-Perlman, D.S. (1992, Winter). The safe classroom. Instructional Development IX: 2, 6 & 8.

Sadker, M. & Sadker, D. (1990, November-December). Sexism in the classroom: From grade school to graduate school. Association for Women in Mathematics Newsletter, 11-14.

Svinicki, M.D. & Dixon, N.M. (1987, Fall). The Kolb model modified for classroom activities. College Teaching, 35: 4, 141-146.

19

I'm Coping As Fast As I Can: Instructing the Instructor at Boston University

J. Christina Smith and Andrea Weinschenk

Mugar Memorial Library — Boston University

With an enrollment of 29,000 students and a 2,500-member faculty, Boston University is the fourth-largest private university in the United States. It has the second-largest international student enrollment in the country. In 1992-93, 4,100 international students from 125 countries attended Boston University.

The university library system is comprised of four major libraries containing 1.8 million volumes and 4 million microforms. Mugar Memorial Library is the main research library. The user population of Mugar Library is large and diverse. From high school students enrolled at Boston University Academy, to doctoral students doing dissertation research, and from international students enrolled in English as a Second Language (ESL) classes, to faculty researching their next book, the patrons of the Mugar Library vary greatly. In addition to serving Boston University library users, Mugar Library's location and

217

open door policy ensure heavy use by the public. Mugar Library is the closest academic library to downtown Boston. It is conveniently located on a major trolley line, serving non-Boston University students and faculty and the greater Boston community at large.

The Bibliographic Services Department of Mugar Library provides reference services, a student-staffed Information Desk, instruction, online services, and interlibrary loan. Bibliographers are responsible for the traditional areas of reference, instruction, online searching, and collection development. Reference, and increasingly, electronic reference, occupies a significant portion of their time. In 1989 our electronic resources consisted of two workstations offering ERIC and PsycLit, and our online catalog. Today we have ten networked workstations with twelve CD-ROM products, five NEXIS terminals, a stand-alone terminal with Business Periodicals Ondisc (BPO), and electronic access to a myriad of other academic library catalogs, and the Boston Library Consortium Union List of Serials and Uncover. Electronic reference tools and questions about their use have increased steadily.

Mugar Library's Reference Desk is staffed from 8:30 am to 10:00 pm Monday through Thursday, 8:30-5 Friday, 9-5 Saturday, and 12-8 Sunday. In the fall of 1990 thirteen bibliographers worked fulltime at Mugar. Two of these individuals also provided reference service at the Science and Engineering Library. Through staff cuts and job vacancies, the number of bibliographers at Mugar had decreased from thirteen to ten by the fall of 1991.

Student assistants work at an Information Desk at the Reference Desk, answering the telephone, answering directional questions, assisting with simple catalog questions, replacing printer paper and ink cartridges, and shelving reference books. Ideally, the Information Desk is staffed all of the hours the Reference Desk is open; however, this is not always possible.

Electronic reference assistants, library school students at nearby Simmons College, are hired on a part time basis to assist the bibliographers with helping patrons with the CD-ROM databases and NEXIS. Hours of coverage are limited, however, leaving reference staff to field all reference inquiries, both print and electronic, as well as general information questions.

The workload of Mugar reference librarians has increased significantly. In the fall of 1989, full-time public services librarians spent an average of eleven hours per week at the Reference Desk, not including evening, weekend, and holiday assignments. Two part-time reference librarians regularly worked one weekend day and two evenings per week. Reference Desk coverage Monday through Friday totaled 160 person-hours. In 1990, statistics at the reference desk call for the scheduling of increased reference coverage during peak daytime hours Monday through Friday. Thus, the reference workload increased to cover an additional 28 hours per week, for a total of 188 hours. By the fall of 1991, reference librarians were spending an average of 15 hours at the reference desk out of a 35-hour week in which they also had instruction and collection development duties.

As for instruction, demand for librarian-led instruction sessions increased, while the number of warm bodies was decreasing. In the fall of 1991, ten librarians conducted eighty-six classes, of which thirty-four, or 39.5 percent were ESL, Rhetoric, and Expository Composition classes. The following semester, these beleaguered librarians conducted eighty-five classes, of which 72 percent, or sixty-one classes, were of the English/ESL variety. Trying to offer 1989 and 1990-level services with a substantially smaller 1992 staff had created a scheduling nightmare. Staff morale was at an all-time low.

The Coordinator of Bibliographic Instruction, who is responsible for assigning and scheduling instructional sessions, also works at the Reference Desk. Dual responsibilities gave the Coordinator different perspectives on the instruction program. When instructors called to schedule an instructional session, they were asked what assignment the library visit was to address. For the introductory Expository Composition, Rhetoric, and some ESL classes a very common assignment was term paper on ''a subject of your choice'' or papers on very broad topics such as ''The City.'' Instructors were routinely asked, ''Can you give specific examples of topics your students will be writing on?'' The subjects ranged from acid rain to acid rock and librarians incorporated research strategies for these topics in their instructional sessions. However, it was not possible to address all the topics in a single visit to the library. While working at the Reference Desk, the Coordinator and other librarians noticed familiar topics addressed in the Expository Composition, Rhetoric, and ESL instruction sessions were recurring as reference questions. There was a flaw in the program. We were devoting time and effort to instruction, but our users were not grasping specific research strategies or even the general principles of library research.

What could be done to change this situation? We only had a summer to devise a plan to (1) alleviate the burden on our librarians and (2) provide more effective instruction for our users. Time constraints prevented us from carrying out an in-depth review of our instruction methods. Our reduced staffing situation precluded assigning additional librarians to each instructional session, thus providing more individual attention. Term paper clinics were also deemed to be a staffing problem and undesirable from a logistics point of view. We had to come up with a solution which could be implemented quickly and did not require more staff or funding. Involving instructors of the Expository Composition, Rhetoric, and ESL classes in introducing users to the basic library skills seemed to be something which could be done in the allotted time using existing library staff. The working name of the program was Instruct the Instructor. Eventually, this became shortened to I^2 (I squared), the name by which it is known today. The first step in implementing the program was to gain administrative approval. Library Administration was well aware of the staffing problem and representatives of the librarians' union (Local 925 of the Service Employees International Union) had spoken to the Director about their concerns regarding the escalating staff workload. The Instruction Committee of the Bibliographic Services Department was reactivated and Committee members drew up a broad outline of how the program would work and the classes it would target. The Coordinator presented this to the Director and approval to create a prototype was granted.

During the summer of 1992, the Instruction Committee met frequently to design the I^2 program. Since our target audience was, for the most part, a group of first-year students, we decided that we would teach the instructors how to give their classes a basic library tour. When an instruction session was requested, we would meet with the instructors one-on-one. The I² sessions would be tailored to each instructor's level of library skills. They would be shown locations of library services, the online catalog, journal indexes (both print and CD-ROM) and the various locations for journals in the library. If needed, we would teach refresher courses to instructors in succeeding semesters. The regularly scheduled reference staff would continue to provide individualized help for students. We would also continue to offer librarian-led instruction for upper level classes which were subject specific, e.g. Psychology 101.

A packet of handouts was created for the instructors. The packet included existing materials and materials we created especially for the program. It includes an outline of an instruction session, library locations and hours, circulation policies, OPAC searching with attention to Library of Congress Subject Headings (LCSH), journal indexes in print and CD-ROM, a glossary and other handouts which instructors may wish to copy and hand out to their classes. It should be noted here that our abdication of the position of ''Handout Supplier to the Masses'' represented a saving in paper, photocopy costs, and staff time. Formerly, a departmental assistant was responsible for making multiple copies of handouts. Now it is up to the instructor to decide what materials she wishes to copy for her class and copying is done in the departmental offices.

When we had created our handouts and had a general plan of action in place, we were ready to launch this new program. In late summer of 1992, when the instructors began calling to arrange instructional sessions for their fall classes, we informed them of the I² program. The need for a new approach to these classes was explained with emphasis on the instructors' ability to interact more closely with their students in the research process. Our staffing situation was another issue worthy of mention. Reactions were mixed. Some instructors went along with the idea more or less willingly; others were opposed and made their opposition known to their department heads. In some cases, instructors had relied for many years on particular librarians to teach their classes and did not want to give up these long-term partnerships. Attempts to circumvent the new program were made. Appeals were sent to Library Administration to reinstate the librarian-led instruction, but the Library maintained its position.

When we meet with instructors, we give them the I² packet, describe the Boston University Libraries and outline the focus of the tour: locations of library services at Mugar Library, and how to find books and journals. The online catalog, Innopac, is the first stop. We do a canned search and suggest that it would be advantageous for the instructor to do the same. Catalog features, such as limit options, reading a call number, and understanding the circulation status line, are covered, as are the LCSH Pertinent packet handouts explaining Innopac searching, LCSH and call number locations.

Our next stop is the index tables. On the way we detour to point out the Reference Desk, Circulation Desk, Photocopy Services, and Reserve. At the index tables we go over the "how to find periodical articles" handout, point out the myriad of paper indexes we have, and show them how a paper index is used. We then move to the CD-ROM workstations, where we explain signup procedures, distribute the list of available CD-ROM databases, and caution the instructors to tell their students that the most appropriate index for their subject may not be computerized. While doing a canned search, we make it clear that the various databases are made by different companies and do not work alike. We explain the importance of using controlled vocabulary (pointing out online and paper thesaurus), and of limiting searches. We stress that the students should talk to us if they have any questions about what database to use and how to use it. Finally, we show how to find a journal by checking the online catalog or the Boston Library Consortium Union List of Serials, consulting the location guide, and going to the appropriate location: Current Periodicals, Microforms, or the stacks. We finish the tour with a trip to Current Periodicals and Microforms, located in the basement.

These are the things we always try to cover to ensure that people can find their way around the library and they know what library services are available. No tour is typical, however, and recent I² tours have included biographical sources, reference books, and Uncover, which is available on our online catalog.

In the two semesters before the I^2 program was instituted (Fall 1991 and Spring 1992), librarians taught a total of 171 classes. Of these, 95 (6 percent) were for the Expository Composition, Rhetoric, and ESL classes. Each of these classes is an hour long; if 0.5 hour (minimum) preparation time is added, the time devoted to these classes comes to 142.5 hours. This represents slightly more than four 35-hour workweeks, a considerable amount of staff time. In the two semesters after I^2 was introduced, librarians taught 101 classes of the 185 classes that were brought to the library, 55 percent of all classes taught. The librarian-led classes included 20 Instruct the Instructor sessions (librarians teaching instructors). These instructors taught the other 84 classes (45 percent). For each Instruct the Instructor session (20), we were getting a return better than four to one, not counting the startup "cost" of the time spent creating the program.

In a very real way, we met one of our objectives: we reduced our teaching load by 59 percent. The total number of classes taught increased slightly (8 percent). At the time of the study, the average Reference Desk assignment was fifteen hours per week. As a result, an average of seventeen classes per librarian have been added over an academic year. These classes were, of course, heavily concentrated in the first seven weeks of each semester. It is easy to see that the demands on staff time were significant. With I^2, the average number of classes per librarian decreased to ten. The amount of time devoted to reference and instruction is still considerable, but staff appreciate the effort to lighten the burden. The classes which staff teach now are more closely associated with their subject areas, although librarians are called upon to assist in large classes in disciplines other than their own. The opportunity to work closely with faculty and students in their subject areas is rewarding.

The number of classes for our target population decreased (ninety-five pre-I^2 vs. eighty-four post-I^2: 11 percent). The decrease seems to be mainly in the ESL classes. One might speculate that the ESL instructors, many of whom are part-time with fulltime positions elsewhere, simply do not have the time to participate in this program. For the Expository Composition and Rhetoric classes, an encouraging change is noted. Some instructors are bringing their classes in for a series of sessions in the library. For example, one instructor devotes one session to finding books on a subject. A second session uses microforms. The final session uses periodical indexes, both print and CD-ROM. With our staffing levels, we would not be able to support this level of instruction.

In spite of our careful planning, we have found several "aberrations." Instructors do not always call to schedule a class with the Coordinator. This can result in traffic jams in the Reference area. For instructors who do call, there is too often a game of "telephone tag." Increased use of e-mail would help to resolve this problem. Instructors try to do "end runs" around the Coordinator to schedule a librarian-led class: feigning ignorance of the I^2 program or withholding the course number are two common ploys. Without warning, instructors will appear at the Reference Desk and ask for several dozen copies of call number location guides or CD-ROM handouts. During an instructor-led class, some instructors will shanghai a librarian at the Reference Desk for assistance with the catalog or a CD-ROM database. It is difficult to extricate oneself from this situation politely. We try to resolve these problems as they arise and to use these glitches as an opportunity to educate instructors so there is no recurrence of the situation.

In the summer of 1993, we interviewed some of the instructors who had participated in the program. While they would all prefer to return to librarian-led instruction, they feel increasingly comfortable bringing classes to the library. They appreciated the opportunity to meet with a librarian one-on-one. On several occasions, instructors have obtained information that was valuable in their own work. Instructors find it difficult to keep abreast of these changes in the library. They all had difficulty with CD-ROM databases, mainly because of limited experience with this technology. The "refresher course" is given most often for I^2 and concentrates on brushing up on CD-ROM. Handouts we have created are distributed by instructors as part of part of the package for their students' use. They did have suggestions for additional handouts, e.g. commonly asked questions and a handout for interpreting and using call numbers. We plan to incorporate some of their suggestions in our enhancements to I^2.

Instruct the Instructor was created, in part, to address the problem of staff workload. At that level, it succeeds. For the foreseeable future, there will not be any large-scale staff increases, but demand for reference service will remain the same or grow. It is clear that we shall have to continue this program and make it as effective as possible. We still do not know if our users have become have become better at grasping basic principles of library research. Our experience calls library instruction into question. Does it work? At what level?

APPENDIX 1

Library Instruction — Mugar Library

Pre I^2

1st semester: Sept. - Dec. 1991
  Total of sessions — 86
  ESL, EN10x, Rhetoric 34 (39.5% of total)

2d semester: Jan. - May 1992
  Total of sessions — 85
  ESL, EN10x, Rhetoric 61 (72% of total)

Total for academic year
  Total of sessions — 171
  ESL, EN10x, Rhetoric 95 (64% of total)

Post I^2

1st semester: Sept. - Dec. 1992
  Total of sessions — 69
  Librn. sessions   47   68%   (I^2: Librn. Instr. = 7)
  Instr. sessions   22   32%

2d semester: Jan. - May 1993
  Total of sessions — 116
  Librn. sessions   54   46.5%   (I^2: Librn. Instr. = 13)
  Instr. sessions   62   53.5%

Total for academic year
  Total of sessions — 185
  Librn. sessions   10   155%   (20 Librn. Instr.)
  Instructor sessions 84   45%

APPENDIX 2

An Introduction to Boston University Library's Resources.

Introduction

  I. Topics to be covered in the session:
     A. Location of library services (1st flr., Current Periodicals &
        Microforms).
     B. Discussion of library services.
     C. How to find books & journal articles in the library.
 II. Boston University Libraries:
     A. Academic libraries: Scope is different than public libraries.
     B. Mugar is the general library of the Boston University Libraries.
        Other libraries include Science & Engineering, Education,
        Law, Medicine and Theology.
     C. Other libraries housed in Mugar include: Music, African
        Studies & Special Collections.

Online Catalog

   I. Online Catalog gives call numbers for book in Mugar and other
      libraries in the Boston University Library system.
  II. It is menudriven.
 III. Search as follows:
      A. Explain the menu choices.
      B. Point out limits (language, date, etc.).
      C. Discuss Library of Congress subject headings. (HANDOUT).
      D. Discuss status of the book (date due, reserve, etc.).
  IV. First floor locations:
      A. Reference/Information Desk (Location guides).
      B. Elevators - North & South.
      C. Circulation Desk (Circulation policy handout).
      D. Reshelving.
      E. Reserve.
      F. Photocopy (include copy card vending machine).

Journal Articles *(Index section of Reference area)*

I. Importance of finding journal articles:
   A. Current.
   B. Coverage of material that is not in book form.
II. Sources for finding journal articles:
   A. Print indexes (paper & microfilm).
   B. Bibliographies.
   C. CD-ROM databases.
   D. Online databases.
III. Print Indexes (Index tables):
   A. Location in the library.
   B. General coverage vs. subject specific coverage.
   C. Scholarly vs. popular.
   D. Some topics may be investigated in several different subject areas.
      (For example, psychological, medical, social, legal aspects of abortion).
   E. How to read citations & abstracts (HANDOUT).
IV. CD-ROM databases (CD-ROM terminals):
   A. What these databases do: Compare to catalog.
   B. It is necessary to know how to use both print & CD-ROM because not all subject areas are represented on CD-ROM.
   C. CD-ROM demo (HANDOUT):
      1. Importance of limiting retrieval.
      2. Controlled vocabulary (where applicable).

Locating Journals in the Library

I. General considerations:
   A. Journal titles and holdings owned by the Boston University Libraries are in the online catalog and may be located by searching for the title of the journal.
   B. Current journals are in Current Periodicals Area (downstairs) in alphabetical order.
   C. Noncurrent journals are bound at the end of each year, given a call number and shelved with books.
   D. Noncurrent journals might also be in microfilm. They will have a call number and will be in the Microfilm Reading Room.
II. Boston Library Consortium Union List of Serials:
   A. Lists other libraries as well as Boston University.
   B. Lists volumes and years owned.
   C. Gives call number for print and microform.

III. Current Periodicals Area (Lower level on the right):
    A. Alphabetical arrangement of journals
    B. Location of newspapers local & international
IV. Microform Reading Room (Lower level on the left):
    A. Journal call numbers are on the drawers.
    B. User locates microfilm:
    C. Microfilm readers have instructions on them. Rdg. Rm. staff are there to assist.
    D. Newspapers do not have call numbers. Need name & date.
    E. Reader/printer will copy film or fiche.
    F. Ask for help if necessary.

20

KAPOW:
The Impact of CD-ROMs
on Bibliographic Instruction

Joan H. Worley
Maryville College

I have studied calligraphy. I begin with that statement only partly for effect; my real objective is to encourage your examination of my topic, the impact of CD-ROMs on bibliographic
instruction, in a broad context. Since our subject is bibliographic
instruction, let's follow the traditional search strategy and begin with an article in a subject encyclopedia in order to get a
bird's eye view of the environment. The encyclopedia I used
is *The Encyclopedia of Quality.*

The history of writing has followed a steady downward
trajectory since 1450. When movable type came along, people re-
acted with horror. They said it was ugly, and indeed it was:
blotchy and too black on the page and certainly less aestetical-
ly pleasing than an illuminated page or manuscript. "Oh well,
use it for trade," they said. So among the early uses of print,
one finds business cards and advertising broadsides. The same

phenomenon can be observed with the introduction of the type-writer, and again, with the computer. At the outset, the letter-forms of both were judged too crude for personal correspondence and used only for business. Today, letters formed by machines are quite acceptable, and one finds calligraphy used for social correspondence only at Buckingham Palace and foreign embassies, along with other vestigial traces of bygone eras, like satin knee britches and shoes with silver buckles.

The contrast between that day and this is blinding. Whether you are looking at the beauty of the letters on the page, the enduring nature of paper (vellum or parchment), the binding, the contents of the book, or the education of youth, the late 20th century suffers in any comparison of quality. This of course, does not include quantity. Our books are poorly printed on self-destructing paper; many are non-books, possessing only transitory recreational value or attraction. Our children are educated under a universal system of public schooling that imparts minimal skills to those who attend well. Few learn to read in depth, fewer still in classical languages. But anyone who will can learn . . . or publish a book.

According to the *Encyclopedia of Quality,* during the last 500 years we have gathered downhill momentum exponentially. When we got to the 20th century, we jumped off the cliff. Quality is not in demand. Convenience sells. Which brings us to CD-ROMs.

CD-ROMs are simply another view of democracy in action.

When we ordered our first CD-ROM index, InfoTrac Academic Index, we dreamed up ways of advertising it on campus. Needless to say to any of you, it needed no advertisement. Students were drawn to it by magnetic force, not by librarians; somehow they found citations without instruction or guidance from us, and yes, managed to locate articles, make photocopies, and depart the library without asking a librarian. CD-ROMs have taken the hocus pocus out of library assignments. Consider what we find necessary to teach when introducing paper indexes. Remember the freshman child you were, and listen to your librarian self: subject headings are in heavy type mumbo jumbo title of article mumbo jumbo first number is volume mumbo jumbo abbreviation front of the volume.

Strangely enough, it is necessary to explicate a citation in a paper index, but when the same information is on screen, our students can absorb and understand the information without any explanation, or at least enough of it to find the article in the bound journal. (I wonder why this is. Maybe students are more receptive to information on screen than in print. Maybe the small type size and the number of citations on a double-page spread of Reader's Guide is offputting, versus the four citations per screen on InfoTrac. Maybe print demands a tenacity they lack.) The point remains: for the first time, students have autonomous control of their library use, and it is CD-ROM indexes that have freed them from the tyranny of their own inadequacy—not knowing, feeling stupid, and having to ask. (Before you demur, let me make plain that I am speaking of student perceptions. Our view of reality may be somewhat different. We may think they still don't know what they ought to know, or that they ought to be asking questions. But "ought" is irrelevant.)

CD-ROMs offer many of the same attractions as other new technologies that we have seen come and go: convenience, speed, compact storage of information, and the allure of newness—"sex appeal." We said many of the same things about microcards, microfiche, microfilm, and assorted other AV tricks; but CD-ROMs are different. Unlike a reader-printer, a projector, or even a VCR, the equipment is easy to use ("You can't break it," we say to students), and more important, Info-Trac, for one, offers hundreds, even thousands of references on freshman topics, and confers instant mastery (or the perception thereof). Instead of another hurdle to climb, the technology is empowering. Suddenly, they don't have to ask.

The effect on libraries and library instruction has been KAPOW.

We are still reeling. Demands for interlibrary loan are off the charts. Should we move our instruction for students to the interlibrary loan office, where they take their printout of 253 articles on suicide? Should we stand by and watch print indexes gather dust? Observing student use of this new indexing technology, librarians have voiced a plethora of concerns. Yes, students love CD-ROMs indexes, but . . .

. . . they use them to the exclusion of other indexes that might be more productive for their topics.

. . . they don't know what they're not getting; they key in just one subject heading, take the printout and run; they get something—anything—and that's all they want. (This may be the most difficult common practice for librarians to accept. We want students to develop critical search skills, to distinguish between the wheat and the chaff, between an article on Toni Morrison in Jet and one in PMLA.)

. . . the number of records or references retrievable on CD-ROM indexes exacerbates their misconception that more is better (or as one student told me recently, "There's never too much." He chose Faulkner for the subject of a short paper for English.)

. . . they are hopelessly heedless in doing their searches—if they get 638 articles on abortion, that's okay, they'll take any 10 or 12, willy nilly.

. . . they don't know what they're doing, really. They have no conceptual understanding of a search process; they don't see how a CD-ROM index fits into a search process or strategy.

. . . they don't even want to know how to use CD-ROMs more efficiently; their eyes glaze over when we try to tell them about full-text features, Boolean searching, or the directory information loaded on the same database.

Librarians worry about the uncritical snatch and grab we see all too often at CD-ROM work stations.[1] We perceive these new library behaviors as loss. (Actually, the behaviors aren't new, but library success using those behaviors is.) We try to do more. We anguish in print, writing, ". . . unless we guide [students] to doing more precise searches, we are doing them a disservice."[2] We are lamenting the loss of illuminated manuscripts in the face of an irresistible new technology.

Our responses to the new technology have been as varied as our libraries.

1. We are adding CD-ROM coverage to our already packed BI presentations.
2. We are substituting CD-ROM instruction for instruction in paper indexes.
3. We are developing CD-ROM point-of-use tools.
4. We are providing CD-ROM rovers for one-on-one point-of-use instruction.
5. We are setting up separate reference service points for CD-ROMs.
6. We are scheduling extracurricular group instruction.
7. We are developing new and ambitious instructional goals and objectives.[3]
8. And, perhaps, needless to say, we are writing articles; articles discussing (with much fervor) the need for more and better instruction, articles describing the methods of instruction for CD-ROMs, articles comparing user satisfaction with various methods of instruction for CD-ROMs, and, as always, articles agonizing over what users don't know and we do.

In short, our professional response to the development of CD-ROM indexing technology is deja vu all over again: we are reliving ancestral stages in the development of BI. Before we go any further in the planning and implementation of new or revised strategies for teaching information skills, I would suggest that we question some of our basic assumptions, the first of which is need. Traditional BI assumed that (1) students needed to know what we were teaching; and (2) students knew they needed to know, because they had assignments requiring the use of unknown library resources. For many undergraduate students, and perhaps for every freshman and sophomore, these assumptions are no longer valid. They no longer have to know what we teach. The information and understanding we offer could be helpful to them, but they don't know that.

In a few years, every arriving freshman will be computer literate (perhaps they are already, at your institution), CD-ROM indexes will have more nearly uniform protocols and command structures, and even the so-called "advanced searching" indexes (PsycLIT, MLA, ERIC, ISI citation indexes, etc.) will be friendlier to users. It is time to re-examine our purpose, recognizing that the environment has changed irrevocably, with profound implications for librarianship. In the past we have thought of ourselves as stewards of information, perhaps as missionaries, and yes, as gatekeepers. The present reality demands that we redefine ourselves. We are stewards of information, still, but we no longer have all the information. We are knowledgeable, helpful, even evangelical, at times, about information; but the gates have been thrown open. Some of our users are getting hold of information we don't even have. In fact, this is happening all the time.

I'd like to digress a bit on this phenomenon. We don't talk about it much, but, in fact, control has traditionally come with our territory. We put little numbers on the books. We keep detailed records of books we own, by author, title, and subjects no normal person would ever think to look under. We have a million persnickety procedures. If you don't follow our rules, you can't have the information. And you have to be quiet about it, and reasonably clean and well-behaved. (The unhappy stereotype of a controlling person—either a fussy wimp of a man who lives with his mother and a small dog, or a disapproving, dried-up woman in lace-up shoes—enforcing rules and saying "Shhh" is not exactly off the wall, in my opinion. I grew up in a neighborhood library with just such a librarian.)

But do admit: librarians have lost control, on both the macro and micro levels. On the macro level, there's an information industry making decisions, mostly by default, that will affect our libraries and our lives more than anything we do, either individually or as professional associations. On the micro level, the CD-ROM, or something even "more better faster," is here to stay. Nobody is going to go back to cursive writing with a quill pen. The Pandora's box of machine print, careless scholarship, and information products that rise or fall according to the bottom line is open.

How should we position ourselves to meet the new century? How should our instructional efforts be focused right now?

Swallow hard, embrace the future, and fight to be heard. Technological change may represent loss, and in fact, I would argue that in many ways it does—especially if it means (as I think it does) relaxing some quality standards for scholarship that faculty and librarians hold dear. It can also mean getting a grip on the information society. Librarians must be involved in the design of systems and software for retrieval. It was 400-500 years after Gutenberg before pagination, indexing, and the like were standardized, and I maintain it was at least partly because there were no librarians making connections between printers, booksellers, and buyers. We must be both loud and articulate advocates for our users. We are the only voice they have.

For the immediate future, and I mean by that, 1994-95, I see three imperatives: we must keep our minds open; be flexible; and stay focused on larger goals above and beyond the activity level. Keeping an open mind is undoubtedly the hardest thing in the world to do. Once BI programs are in place, they have a tendency to roll on, semester after semester, and our thinking about them tends to get codified, or set in grooves that are not receptive to change. I look forward to seeing a greater variety of BI responses to CD-ROMs on campuses. I hope that at least one research library will try some wild and crazy, new and different instruction—perhaps rely entirely on informal, one-on-one instruction, with no classroom presentations.

Flexibility requires us to think in terms of levels of need, or perhaps, size of appetite. What freshmen want and what graduate students want are very different things. Ditto 18-year-old community college students and continuing education (adult) learners. Age and stage of our constituent groups will determine how much and what kind of instruction we offer. If your students are high-scoring achievers who prefer print on paper, go for it: teach information search strategies, in depth and in detail. However, I think most of us will be re-examining what and how we are teaching freshmen, and observing their reactions very closely. The days of freshman BI as we know it today may be numbered. Logic suggests that in the near future we will be devoting to upper-division and graduate students considerable energies and resources currently expended on freshmen.

It is tempting to discuss in detail various instructional

responses to CD-ROM technologies in libraries: how librarians are developing new instructional activities and programs, working with teaching faculty to design instruction that's on target for specific information needs, and educating faculty to CD-ROM and other technologies. The activity level is always fun. We compare notes and get practical ideas to try out at home. However, I would suggest that every librarian needs to be focused first on questions of educational program and outcomes. Librarians have an unusual perspective on the educational process with the prospect of new equations of knowledge and power. We should be reporting our observations and articulating our concerns to programmers, manufacturers, and distributors of software; to representatives of local, state, and federal government; and of course, to college and university faculty and administrators.

Keep in mind that, traditionally, faculty assignments have driven student library use, and to that extent, faculty have exercised ''control'' of the use of information resources by students, not unlike librarians' control of access. Even as we speak, traditional relationships between the thing read, the student, the professor, and the librarian are changing and will continue to change. Many of us are discussing the impact of new technologies on campus with teaching faculty, at both abstract and concrete levels; I think all of us need to be doing this. There is a wide range of comfort/discomfort, and experience/inexperience with telecommunication among faculty on college and university campuses, and different sets of values at work. We can help.

In this time of technological flux, perhaps only librarians can ascertain needs of the student and the professor; make useful information connections between them, with print, nonprint, or virtual resources; and work creatively with faculty and administrators to forge a new information literacy. With a quill pen in one hand and a mouse in the other, librarians have a transcending, connecting power. Let's keep it focused on engineering design and planning, on the big picture, and for Heaven's sake, let's use it.

ENDNOTES

1. For a range of opinions from librarians, see: Tenopir, Carol, "Online Databases," Library Journal 117.6 (April 1, 1992), 96-98.

2. Jacobson, Trudi E., "All I Need Is the Computer," Reference Librarian 38 (1992), 222.

3. Nipp, Deanna, "Back to Basics: Integrating CD-ROM Instruction With Standard User Education," Research Strategies 9 (Winter, 1991), 41-7.

Conference Summary

Joseph Boisse and Carla Stoffle
University of California at Santa Barbara/
University of Arizona

The success of a conference like this is difficult to gauge. The participants clearly enjoyed the ambiance and the locale. Even casual observation of the participants during coffee breaks, the luncheon, and the all-conference reception showed that a great deal of networking was going on. The organizers exceeded the attendance target they had set, and everything went off according to plan. But the real success or failure of such a gathering is not measured by these criteria alone.

The most important question that can be asked to assess the value of the conference is: what will happen when the participants go back to their home institutions? And, of course, it is not possible to answer that question up front. An evaluation of any conference really ought to include follow-up questionnaires to the participants a year or two afterwards. The main goal of the questionnaire would be to ascertain if they put into practice any of the ideas they picked up here.

In conducting the conference wrap-up session, Stoffle and Boisse decided to query the participants about ideas or thoughts that had caught their fancies during the day-and-a-half meeting. In a lively session, some twenty ideas were mentioned. They range across a broad spectrum of instructional issues: some refer to specific programmatic suggestions, others call attention to principles which might guide our efforts, and still others are quick reminders that there is always something new for us to learn.

The following items are listed in the order they were actually discussed during the wrap-up session.

1. There is an historical continuum to what we do: it has progressed from BI (bibliographic instruction) to LI (library instruction) to DI (document instruction) on to II (information instruction).

2. Bring technical services people into public service areas. Break down the barriers that have been set up over the years in our libraries between these two services. Technical services staff frequently have specialized backgrounds that can help us provide better service to our clientele, and we're missing a potentially rich resource if we ignore these folks.

3. Look at library organization charts in new ways—from the ground up—and develop a new language to describe them. In the new world of higher education it is important that the libraries change along with our parent institutions. In redesigning our libraries we should begin by learning about our clientele, our users, and make that knowledge the basis for any organizational rationale.

To facilitate this effort, we should strive to break away from the bonds of traditional language. Let's find new ways to talk about what we do and how we are organized to do it so we will not be limited by the accumulated baggage of historical terms as they relate to academic libraries.

4. Partnerships with other constituencies need to be pursued aggressively. We must look beyond the library and even beyond those campus groups with whom we traditionally have formed alliances. Our efforts to link up with previously ignored campus units can help us reach new constituencies, campus groups that might otherwise not benefit from the information resources of the library.

5. Before we can have collaboration on the campus, we have to break down barriers within the library and between library departments. This ties in with the third item mentioned above. For the most part academic libraries are organized along very rigid lines and there is relatively little communication (sometimes even less cooperation) between/among the various camps. No matter how much effort we put into reaching out to campus constituencies, if we don't first address the challenge of creating a real team within the library our efforts will be less than successful.

6. Establish links with other non-instructional units on campus. Historically, libraries have worked primarily to establish links with faculty. It was suggested that we have a lot in common with other campus units, frequently non-instructional, which also work to improve the academic experience of the students.

7. Maintain the human link in the library to help students deal with technology. It's fatuous, if not dangerous, to assume that technology will solve all library service problems. We may be expecting too much of our clientele, at least in the beginning stages of their computerized experiences. We must make every effort to help them make their transition into the technological world of information retrieval a smooth one.

8. Teams, and the way we put them in place, are very different from committees or task forces, but they are a new and effective management strategy for problem-solving. They are an excellent example of the breaking away from traditional structures and terminology and trying out new approaches for meeting challenges within the library.

9. It's important to measure outcomes. We must be able to demonstrate our programs are making a difference in students' lives.

10. User independence, achieved using everything from signs to electronic gateways, is crucial. If we have a long range goal to move our users towards independence in their search for information, we must look at the inanimate functions of our libraries (i.e., signage) to remove barriers from patrons use of the facility.

11. Serving remote constituencies—how do we deal with

these groups? Many of our institutions are involved with distance learning. What about information resources? What are we doing to ensure that these members of the academic community are not information poor?

12. We are doing more than just "coping." There are lots of creative solutions to downsizing that are being tried as librarians see opportunities rather than just obstacles in reduced budgets.

13. This is the best time to go through radical change since the financial crisis makes it easier for people to accept it. Radical problems call for radical solutions. The more difficult our financial problems, the more we must be creative in identifying solutions. Let's seize the opportunity created by the current fiscal crisis to introduce change.

14. Don't reinvent the wheel—lift others' ideas. This is an obvious strategy to follow, since none of us has time NOT to steal ideas. This kind of collegial borrowing can be one of the major benefits of attending conferences like this one.

15. Make vendors responsible for instruction in their tools. Put pressure on them to create better products. Too often vendors dump a new product on us without making any effort to develop instructional materials in its use. They know only, too well, that librarians will take up this challenge. As a group, we must let vendors know that they need to assume some of the responsibility for developing instructional materials for their products, or we won't buy them!

16. Don't forget those who have no on ramp to the information highway. We have a responsibility to a very broad audience, to the have nots as well as to the haves. This is a problem with enormous implications and the caution is very timely. In any one of our institutions there are many individuals who, for whatever reason, do not have access to the information highway. We still have a responsibility to provide them with the best possible information services.

17. More training sessions for librarians to learn to teach are needed (we need good sessions developed from the experience of those who have taught successfully). The point here is that teaching is not some innate ability we can turn on with the press of a button. Good teaching is a skill that can be developed and must be cultivated.

18. Many participants noted that they networked with others throughout the two days and picked up all kinds of new ideas they're taking back to their home institutions. (This is precisely why we put on this conference!)

19. We must see the library as a learning organization—to get better we must learn from ours and others' mistakes. Every experience, whether ours or somebody elses, should make us more effective. This applies to both organizations and individuals.

20. Remember the maxim of "good enough" that Barbara Quint espoused. Trying for ultimate perfection in every project is self-defeating, inefficient, and counter-productive. Aim for doing something well enough to get the message across, then move on to the next project.

Index